Exploring Measurements

Exploring
Measurements

Peter Barbella

James Kepner

Richard Scheaffer

DALE SEYMOUR PUBLICATIONS

Project Editor: Katarina Stenstedt
Production Director: Janet Yearian
Production Coordinator: Leanne Collins
Design Manager: Jeff Kelly
Cover Design: Terry Guyer

Dale Seymour Publications is an imprint of Addison-Wesley's Alternative
Publishing Group.

ISBN 0-86651-639-5
Order Number DS21206

1 2 3 4 5 6 7 8 9–ML–97 96 95 94 93

This book is printed
on recycled paper.

DALE
SEYMOUR
PUBLICATIONS
P.O. BOX 10888
PALO ALTO, CA 94303

CONTENTS

PREFACE

Exploring Measurements is the fifth booklet in the Quantitative Literacy Series, which was developed by a joint task force consisting of the National Council of Teachers of Mathematics and the American Statistical Association for the purpose of providing materials on statistics and probability appropriate for secondary schools. A brief review of the other four booklets of the series will help place this one in proper perspective.

Exploring Data presents a number of techniques, mostly graphical, for use in studying patterns and departures from patterns that might be observed in real data. Different ways of presenting data and relationships between sets of data are described.

Exploring Probability focuses on the language and use of elementary probability ideas, concentrating on probability as a long-run relative frequency that can be approximated through data or modeled theoretically. The practical use of probability to make decisions is emphasized throughout.

The Art and Techniques of Simulation builds upon the relative frequency notion of probability to establish a simulation model for assessing real probability problems. This approach allows students to study probability and expected value problems of a realistic nature, even when the construction of a theoretical model would be well beyond their capabilities.

Exploring Surveys and Information from Samples shows ways of estimating the chances that particular events will occur and of estimating how accurate the predictions are likely to be. The common opinion poll serves as the major source of applications for relating this work to the real world.

Building upon this background, *Exploring Measurements* extends the idea of estimating proportions to the problem of estimating means. The book begins with the study of measures of center and spread for measurement data (for example, ages of teachers, prices of houses, batting averages of baseball players, and SAT and ACT scores). These ideas are then used to describe the sampling distribution of sample means. Confidence-interval estimates of population means are developed in a way that parallels their development for proportions in earlier work.

Study of the five booklets in the Quantitative Literacy Series will take you through the notions of describing data, obtaining representative data through random sampling, and using sample data to describe certain population characteristics by estimating proportions or means. These are the building blocks of quantitative literacy, which is the ability to intelligently describe data and correctly use data in making decisions.

I. SUMMARIZING A DATA SET

Introduction

There are a variety of ways in which we can learn about the world around us. Words can be used to describe living things, the earth's features, or what makes an airplane fly. Unfortunately, few words have an exact meaning. A person living in the tropics might consider 50° F (Fahrenheit) to be "cold" while a person living in the arctic probably would not describe such a day as being cold at all. Numbers, however, have meanings that are more precise than words. For this reason, when it is feasible, numbers are often relied upon to describe the world. Numerical information is called *data*. Virtually everyone, not just scientists and researchers, uses data to communicate ideas and information. Consequently, our ability to comprehend the world around us often depends in part upon our understanding of data and our ability to analyze them. The branch of study that deals with the collection and analysis of data is called *statistics*.

In this section, you will use numbers and easy-to-make graphs to summarize data so their message may be more readily understood. You might ask, "Why should we settle for a summary of the data if we have all the data? Isn't something lost in a summary?" Yes, something is lost. However, imagine looking through the dozens, hundreds, or even thousands of numbers that might be contained in a data set. It would be extremely difficult, as well as time consuming, to look through that many numbers and get an understanding of whatever phenomenon was being measured.

The Grand Total and the Mean

Below are the seating capacities for each of the 26 major-league baseball parks during the 1992 season.

Seating Capacity in the Major League Baseball Parks	
American League	Seating Capacity
Baltimore Orioles' Park at Camden Yards	48,000
Boston Red Sox's Fenway Park	33,925
California Angels' Anaheim Stadium	64,593
Chicago White Sox's Comiskey Park	44,177
Cleveland Indians' Municipal Stadium	74,483
Detroit Tigers' Stadium	52,416
Kansas City Royals' Stadium	40,625
Milwaukee Brewers' County Stadium	53,192
Minnesota Twins' Hubert H. Humphrey Metrodome	55,883
New York Yankees' Stadium	57,545
Oakland Athletics' Alameda County Stadium	47,313
Seattle Mariners' Kingdome	59,702
Texas Rangers' Arlington Stadium	43,521
Toronto Blue Jays' Skydome	50,516

Continued on next page

Seating Capacity in the Major League Baseball Parks, *continued*	
National League	Seating Capacity
Atlanta Braves' Fulton County Stadium	52,013
Chicago Cubs' Wrigley Field	38,710
Cincinnati Reds' Riverfront Stadium	52,952
Houston Astros' Astrodome	54,816
Los Angeles Dodgers' Stadium	56,000
Montreal Expos' Olympic Stadium	43,739
New York Mets' Shea Stadium	55,601
Philadelphia Phillies' Veterans Stadium	62,382
Pittsburgh Pirates' Three Rivers Stadium	58,729
St. Louis Cardinals' Busch Stadium	56,627
San Diego Padres' Jack Murphy Stadium	59,700
San Francisco Giants' Candlestick Park	62,000

Source: *The Sporting News 1992 Baseball Yearbook.*

Which league has a greater seating capacity in its ball parks, the American League or the National League? To answer this question, it might seem that we would simply add up all the seating capacities of the ball parks for each league and compare the totals.

Total Ball Park Seating Capacity	
American League	725,891
National League	653,269

From these figures, it appears that the American League parks have a greater seating capacity—and, strictly speaking, this is true. However, this method of comparison is unfair because the American League has 14 parks while the National League has only 12. Taking the totals would be fair only if each league had the same number of parks. How can we make a more fair comparison?

We cannot arbitrarily remove two parks from the American League because the choice of parks would affect the results. If we removed two of the larger parks from the American League, the comparison would be biased against that league; if we removed two of the American League's smaller parks, the comparison would be biased against the National League. Removing parks is not the answer. Obviously, we cannot add parks to the National League, either. How then can we make a more fair comparison?

A solution to this dilemma would be to take the total seating capacity of all the American League parks and divide it equally among the 14 parks. This number would tell us the average seating capacity per park. We could do the same for the National League. Then, even though the number of parks differ, we would have a fair basis for comparison.

Here are the calculations, rounded to the nearest whole number:

American: 725,891/14 = 51,849
National: 653,269/12 = 54,439

These numbers indicate that if the seats were divided equally among all the parks in each league, the National League parks would seat more spectators, even though American League parks have the higher total seating capacity.

The calculation we did here produced the average capacity for a park in each league. This average is called a *mean* and it is computed by dividing the grand total of all the data by the number of separate data elements used to get the total. Using a calculator to compute a mean makes your work a lot easier!

Application 1

Summarizing Data Using Totals and Means

Look at the following two sets of data. Then answer the questions after the second set.

The Civil Aeronautics Board (CAB) hears complaints from the public about domestic airlines. This table shows the type and number of complaints the CAB received during the first six months of 1980.

Nature of Complaint	Number of Complaints
Late or canceled flight	2,265
Baggage (lost, delayed, damaged)	1,852
Rudeness from personnel	1,402
Failure to provide expected refunds	978
Overbooking of seats	957
Problems with fares	655
Reservation/ticket problems	601
Smoking on the plane	301
Misleading advertising	111
Inadequate provision for passengers with special needs	90
Other matters	761

Source: *U/S: A Statistical Portrait of the American People*, p. 271.

3

The next table shows the costs of some brands and models of compact-disc players.

Brand	Price
Onkyo Integra DX–706	$400
Sony ES CDP–X222ES	370
Denon DCD–970	335
Yamaha CDX–750	300
Technics SL–PS900	330
Proton AC–422	330
Luxman DZ–122	425
Pioneer Elite PD–41	560
Harmon/Kardon HD7500II	265
NAD 5440	510
Carver SD/A–450	470
Nakamichi 4	330
Onkyo DX–702	185
Kenwood DP–2030	150
Philips CD40	150
Pioneer PD–5700	150
Sony CDP–491	145
Technics SL–PG300	135
JVC XL-V241TN	135
Magnavox CDB–502	130
Sherwood CD–3010R	160
Sears LXI	120
Optimus CD–1750	120
Sharp DX-R250	130

Source: *Consumer Reports*, March 1992, p. 176.

1. Calculate the grand total for the airline complaint data. What does this number tell you about the data?

2. Calculate the mean for the compact-disc-player data. What does this number tell you about the data?

3. Does the mean of the airline complaint data provide you with meaningful information? Why or why not?

4. Does the grand total for the compact-disc-player data provide you with meaningful information? Why or why not?

5. What do your responses to questions 3 and 4 tell about numbers we may use to summarize data?

The following table lists the number of wins for each team in the National Basketball Association at a point about two-thirds of the way into the 1991–92 season.

Eastern Conference	Wins	Western Conference	Wins
Chicago	44	Portland	37
Cleveland	35	Utah	37
New York	33	Golden State	35
Detroit	31	Phoenix	33
Boston	30	San Antonio	31
Atlanta	26	L.A. Lakers	29
Miami	25	Seattle	28
Milwaukee	25	Houston	27
Philadelphia	25	L.A. Clippers	27
Indiana	24	Denver	20
Washington	18	Dallas	16
Charlotte	17	Minnesota	10
Orlando	13		

Source: *New York Times*, 23 February 1992

6. On the basis of the data above, which conference would you rate as better, the Eastern or Western? Explain your answer.

Measures of Center

The U.S. Bureau of the Census periodically prepares the *Statistical Abstract of the United States,* a document that divides the country into nine population regions. The following table lists the states in the Mountain and Pacific regions with their 1990 populations.

Populations of States in Two Regions of the United States (population in millions; data from 1990 census)			
Mountain Region	Population	Pacific Region	Population
Arizona	3.7	Alaska	0.5
Colorado	3.3	California	29.9
Idaho	1.0	Hawaii	1.1
Montana	0.8	Oregon	2.8
Nevada	1.2	Washington	4.9
New Mexico	1.5		
Utah	1.7		
Wyoming	0.5		

Source: *Statistical Abstract of the United States,* 1991, p. 20.

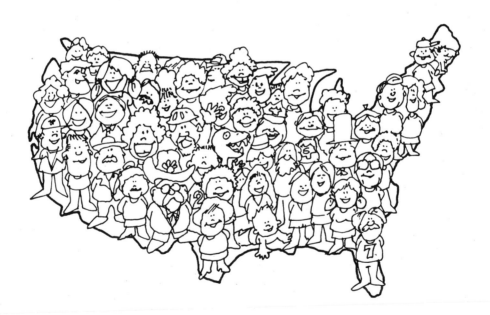

To compare the relative population size of the Mountain states and Pacific states, we might find the mean population of the states in each region, as follows (rounded to the nearest 100,000):

Region	Mean Population
Mountain	1.7 million
Pacific	7.8 million

These means seem to tell us that the Pacific states are considerably more populous than the Mountain states. Does this appear to be true? Are these means good indicators of the average populations of the states in each region? More generally, when is a mean a good "measure of center"?

A population of 1.7 million people—the mean population of the Mountain states—is relatively small. On the whole, it is true that the states in the Mountain region have small populations. Only Arizona and Colorado, each with more than 3 million people, might be considered to have medium-sized populations. Therefore, the mean is a fairly good indicator of the population size of the Mountain states.

For the Pacific states, however, the mean population is approximately 7.8 million. A look back at the data shows that none of the Pacific states has a population that is anywhere near this size. Populations are well below the mean in four of the five states, and California's population exceeds the mean by more than 20 million. Washington, the state whose population is closest to the mean, still has a population that differs from the mean by 2.9 million people. By contrast, the greatest difference between the mean and the actual population of any one state in the Mountain region is just 2 million.

Clearly, the mean is a much better indicator of the population of the individual states in the Mountain region than it is of the individual states in the Pacific region. Is there a different measure of center that is a better indicator of the average population size in both regions?

The *median* is another average, or measure of center. It is the middle value in a data set when the data are ordered low to high or high to low. For example, the populations of the Pacific states ordered from high to low are as follows:

29.9 million
4.9 million
2.8 million
1.1 million
0.5 million

Given these five values, the third value, 2.8 million, is the median because it is the middle number. What if a data set has an even number of data elements so that there is no middle value? For such a data set, the median is the midpoint between the two centermost data elements. For example, look at the ordered data for the Mountain states.

3.7 million
3.3 million
1.7 million
1.5 million
1.2 million
1.0 million
0.8 million
0.5 million

The two data elements in the middle are 1.5 million and 1.2 million. The midpoint between these two is 1.35 million. Thus, 1.35 million is the median population of the Mountain states.

To calculate a median, do the following:

a. Order the data elements, either from low to high or high to low.

b. If the number of data elements is odd, the median is the middle data element.

c. If the number of data elements is even, the median is the midpoint between the two centermost data elements.

For our state population data, is the median any better than the mean at describing the "average state size" in each region? The chart below compares the means and medians (in millions) for the two regions.

Region	Mean	Median
Mountain	1.7	1.35
Pacific	7.8	2.80

Looking at the two measures of center for the Mountain states, we see there is not a large difference between them. Both the mean and the median are good indicators of the population of individual states in this region. For the Pacific states, however, the median is a much better measure of center than the mean because it is closer to most of the populations of the individual states.

This can be illustrated graphically by the use of a *line plot*. A line plot is simply a number line with dots, X's, or some other suitable symbol placed above the line to designate the elements in a data set. For example, the populations of the Mountain states and Pacific states could be illustrated on number lines as below.

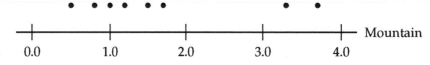

Line Plot of Populations of Mountain States (in millions)

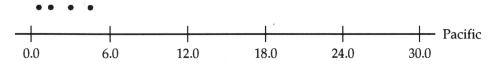

Line Plot of Populations of Pacific States (in millions)

It is quite clear from these line plots that the mean of 1.7 million for the Mountain states is a good measure of the center, while the mean of 7.8 million for the Pacific states is not a good measure of the center.

Here is another way to get a visual sense of the suitability of the mean as a measure of center in any given case: We can graph a line plot of the *differences* or *deviations* between each data element and the mean. For the Mountain states, these differences are as follows:

	Population	Mean	Difference
Arizona	3.7	1.7	2.0
Colorado	3.3	1.7	1.6
Idaho	1.0	1.7	−0.7
Montana	0.8	1.7	−0.9
Nevada	1.2	1.7	−0.5
New Mexico	1.5	1.7	−0.2
Utah	1.7	1.7	0.0
Wyoming	0.5	1.7	−1.2

You can calculate the differences for the Pacific states in the same way. Line plots of the differences would look like this:

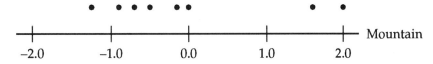

Line Plot of (DATA—MEAN) for Mountain States (differences in millions)

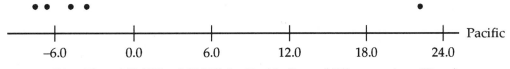

Line Plot of (DATA—MEAN) for Pacific States (differences in millions)

The relationship between the mean and the individual data elements comes in clearer focus in these last two graphs. A dot at zero indicates that the original data element *equals* the mean. The farther a dot falls from zero, the farther the corresponding data element is from the mean. Thus, we can see that all the data elements for the Mountain states cluster fairly close to the mean (all *within* 2 million), while all the data elements for the Pacific states are more than 2 million *away from* their mean.

This example illustrates an important difference between the mean and the median as measures of center. The mean is much more sensitive to the magnitude of each data element in the set than is the median. One very large or very small data element can have a dramatic impact on the mean, especially if there are only a few elements in the data set. The median, however, is not so easily swayed. The median population of the Pacific states would remain 2.8 million regardless of how large the population of California or how small the population of Alaska happened to be.

Can we say, in general, which is a better measure of center, the mean or the median? No, because it depends on the situation. Here is another illustration. In a given year, a major commercial airline typically might experience zero or one fatal crash. The median of the number of crashes per day that year would be zero. If the airline were to experience a fatal crash every week the following year, that would certainly represent an alarming and unacceptable increase in fatal crashes. Yet the median of the number of crashes per day would remain unchanged, still equaling zero. Clearly, in this case, the mean would be the better measure of center. Indeed, the median of the number of crashes per day would be quite misleading.

Here is another example. In 1985, the University of Virginia polled its 1984 graduates to gather data on, among other matters, major in college and current salary. It was discovered that history majors had the highest mean salary among all majors. But, one of the history majors was Ralph Sampson, a professional basketball player earning a six- or seven-figure salary in his first year after graduation, thereby greatly inflating the mean. In this situation, the median would have given a more accurate indication of the typical salary of 1984 graduates of the University of Virginia who had been history majors.

These examples indicate how critical it is to understand the nature of both the mean and the median when exploring data sets.

Application 2

Using The Mean and Median to Locate the Center of a Data Set

1. Three sets of data follow. For each set, do the following:

   a. Calculate the mean.

   b. Calculate the median.

c. Decide if the mean is a good or a poor measure of center.

d. Decide if the median is a good or a poor measure of center.

e. Draw a line plot of the data. What does the line plot reveal about our two measures of center?

f. Subtract the mean from each data element and draw a line plot of the resulting differences. How would you interpret this line plot?

Data Set 1

Following are the number of national parks found in 17 developed nations.

Nation	Number of National Parks
Australia	239
Austria	4
Belgium	1
Canada	70
Denmark	1
France	10
Germany	13
Ireland	1
Italy	5
Japan	37
Netherlands	21
Norway	15
Spain	3
Sweden	26
Switzerland	1
United Kingdom	19
United States	252

Source: *The Book of Numbers,* pp. 38–39.

Data Set 2

Following are the number of pages in each issue of *National Geographic* magazine published in 1988.

Issue	Pages
January	156
February	138
March	128
April	128
May	144
June	144
July	130
August	140
September	164
October	178
November	154
December	182

Source: *National Geographic*, vol. 173–174.

Data Set 3

A family in Madison, Wisconsin, has six members, including two dogs. The ages of the family members are listed below.

Member	Age
Dad	36
Mom	33
Skipper	10
Jenny	7
David	3
Lisa	1

2. The tiny, oil-rich nation of Kuwait has one of the highest per-capita (per-person) incomes (mean income) of any nation in the world. However, before the dramatic increase in oil prices in the 1970s, much of this nation's wealth was concentrated in the hands of a privileged few, while many Kuwaitis went without basic necessities, such as running water. Which measure of center—the mean or the median—do you believe would be best for describing each of the following situations? Explain your answers.

    a. The income of a "typical" Kuwaiti.

    b. The overall wealth in the nation of Kuwait.

3. Find a newspaper or magazine article that contains a mean value. Find an article that contains a median value (it could be the same article that contains the mean value). Underline the words *mean* and *median*. Write a sentence or two describing the data set(s) that each measure represents. Briefly discuss how well you believe each measure of center represents its data set.

Application 3

Means, Means, Means

As you have seen, means are commonly used to summarize a set of measurements. You should be aware, however, that means can be calculated in many ways, and it is not uncommon to see means calculated by inappropriate methods. Always keep in mind that a mean is a total divided by the number of units on the scale to be reported.

Let's try a simple example to make this point clear. Suppose data show that household A contains three people and spent $180 for food during the past week. Household B contains four people and spent $200 on food during the past week. How do you find the mean amount spent on food per *household* during the past week? In terms of household units, the denominator of the mean is 2; and, therefore, the answer is ($180 + $200)/2 = $190. Suppose, instead, we want to find the mean amount spent *per person*. Now, the denominator of the mean is 7 and the answer is ($180 + $200)/7 = $54.28. Note that the mean per person in Household A is $60 and the mean per person in Household B is $50. The overall mean per person is *not* the simple average of these two means. Why not?

The following activities are designed to provide experience in working with means in situations for which the denominators might change from time to time.

Instructions

Compute appropriate means in the situations outlined below.

1. On a four-point grading scale (A = 4, B = 3, C = 2, D = 1, E = 0) a student has an A in a three-credit course, a B in a five-credit course and a C in a four-credit course. What is the student's grade point average (GPA) for this term?

2. Find your GPA for the last term of school that you completed. What would that GPA be if you had taken one more course and received a grade of B?

3. For your favorite brand of cola, find the current prices of three different sizes at the local supermarket. Compute the price per ounce for each size separately. Then, compute the mean price per ounce for all three sizes taken together (that is, if you bought one of each of the three sizes, how much would you be paying per ounce?)

4. Record the number of miles driven and the number of gallons of gasoline used to fill the tank for three fill-ups after the next fill-up of the family car. (Be sure to begin with a full tank. Why?) Compute the mean miles-per-gallon for your car. Discuss at least two possible ways to do this and decide which is the better way.

5. The following data show the box score for a National Basketball Association game between Los Angeles and Dallas. The first pair of numbers is the number of goals made from the field and the number of attempts, the second pair is the number of foul shots made and the number of attempts, and the third number represents the total points scored. Thus, Worthy (L.A.) made 6 goals out of 10 attempts and 3 foul shots out of 4 attempts for a total of 15 points (some field goals are from 3-point range).

   a. Calculate the percentage of field goals (baskets) made for each player.

   b. Calculate the L.A. field-goal percentage made as a team and compare the result to the Dallas field-goal percentage made as a team. Is the team field-goal percentage the simple average of the player's percentages? Why or why not?

   c. Repeat the instructions for (a) and (b) substituting "foul shot" for "field goal."

L.A. Lakers (106)			
Worthy	6–10	3–4	15
Green	4–8	12–13	20
Divac	8–13	3–4	20
Scott	8–13	3–4	20
Johnson	6–12	7–7	21
Thompson	1–6	1–2	3
Teagle	2–9	0–2	4
Smith	1–4	1–2	3
Campbell	0–0	0–0	0
Totals	36–73	30–38	106
Dallas (92)			
McCray	9–16	1–1	19
White	4–10	0–0	8
Donaldson	5–10	0–0	10
Harper	9–24	4–4	24
Blackman	4–17	1–1	11
English	2–5	0–0	4
Williams	6–10	0–0	12
Davis	1–6	0–0	2
Upshaw	1–2	0–0	2
Totals	41–100	6–6	92

6. Study the table on United States Census data and answer the questions below.

   a. Can you reproduce the U.S. unemployment rate (5.5) from the unemployment rates of the four regions? How?

   b. Approximately how many crimes were reported for the Northeast in 1988?

   c. What is the 1988 crime rate for the Northeast and Midwest taken together?

   d. What is the 1988 per-capita income for the South and West taken together?

   e. Pose two additional questions that involve means and that can be answered with the data in this table.

Selected Data—Regions and States							
Region	Total (mil.)	Percent changed 1980–90	Metro-politan area pop. 1988 (%)	Crime rate* 1988	Unemp-loyment rate 1988 (%)	Personal income per capita 1988 ($)	Retail sales per house-hold 1988 ($)
U.S.	248.7	9.8	77.1	5,664	5.5	16,489	17,891
Northeast	50.8	3.4	88.3	5,006	4.0	19,214	19,188
Midwest	59.7	1.4	71.1	4,873	5.8	15,989	17,104
South	85.4	13.4	70.3	6,093	6.1	14,793	17,500
West	52.8	22.3	84.1	6,543	5.6	17,190	18,177

*Per 100,000 population.

Source: U.S. Census Bureau.

Discussion

Compare your results on each of the questions above with those of other class members. Are there differences of opinion on the proper way to compute the means?

Medians, Medians, Medians

The median is an appropriate measure of the center for some data sets, especially those where a line plot of the data is not symmetric (data sets of this type are frequently said to be *skewed*). A median is usually easy to calculate—involving only counting—and has a particularly simple interpretation (half the data are below the median and half are above it). For these and other reasons, medians are often used as summary measures for data sets in printed media, such as newspapers.

As in the case of means, you must be careful to calculate the correct median for the situation at hand and to compare medians on a fair basis. This application is designed to study how various medians may be calculated and compared within the same problem and how medians can be approximated from frequency tables.

Instructions

1. The following table gives the total tax revenues, in billions, and per-capita tax revenues for selected countries in 1988.

Country	Total[a]	Per Capita[b]
United States	1,409.2	5,721
Australia	80.9	4,893
Austria	53.3	7,015
Belgium	69.3	7,014
Canada	169.4	6,529
Denmark	56.0	10,897
Finland	39.9	8,068
France	421.4	7,542
Greece	18.8	1,883
Ireland	13.5	3,810
Italy	307.9	5,360
Japan	903.5	7,368
Luxembourg	3.3	8,739
Netherlands	109.9	7,446
New Zealand	15.8	4,765
Norway	42.8	10,159
Portugal	14.4	1,476
Spain	113.1	2,900
Sweden	100.5	11,914
Switzerland	59.6	8,958
Turkey	16.2	299
United Kingdom	306.7	5,372

[a]In billions of dollars.   [b]In dollars.

Source: *1991 Statistical Abstract of the U.S.*, p. 846.

a. Find the median total tax revenue. To which country does it belong? How far is the United States away from this median?

b. Find the median per-capita tax revenue. To which country does it belong? How far is the United States away from the median?

c. Construct line plots for the sets of data in the table. Mark the location of the United States on each.

d. When going from total to per-capita tax revenues, did any countries switch from below to above the median? If so, which one(s)? Did any countries switch from above to below the median? If so, which one(s)?

e. If you were trying to construct an argument against higher taxes in the United States, which data set would you use? Why?

f. If you were a resident of Norway, how might you argue against higher taxes?

2. Use the data table "Education in the Sunbelt" to answer the following:

a. Find the median high-school graduation rate for the Sunbelt states, for the other populous states, and for all 23 states listed. How do the three medians compare?

b. How could you make use of medians to explain Florida's position among the Sunbelt states and relative to other populous states?

c. Answer questions (a.) and (b.) after replacing "high-school graduation rate" with "average salary for teachers."

d. Answer questions (a.) and (b.) after replacing "high school graduation rate" with "current expenditure per pupil."

e. On which of the three measures used above does Florida look best among the Sunbelt states? On which does Florida look best relative to the other populous states?

Education in the Sunbelt						
Attainment, 1980[a]			Public elementary and secondary schools			
State	Percent age high school graduates	Percent age college graduates	Enroll-ment rate fall 1985[b]	Average salary of teachers 1986–1987 ($1,000)	Current expendi-ture per pupil in ADA 1986–1987[c]	Doctoral scientists and engi-neers per 100,000 persons 1985[d]
Sunbelt states						
Florida	66.7	14.9	87.4	23.8	4,056	85
Alabama	56.5	12.2	89.2	23.5	2,610	104
Arizona	72.4	17.4	90.6	26.3	2,784	144
Arkansas	55.5	10.8	91.9	20.0	2,795	(NA)
California	73.5	19.6	90.6	31.2	3,751	209
Georgia	56.4	14.6	89.9	24.2	3,167	107
Louisiana	57.7	13.9	83.6	21.3	3,237	118
Mississippi	54.8	12.3	82.6	19.6	2,534	(NA)
New Mexico	68.9	17.6	89.7	24.0	3,537	366
North Carolina	54.8	13.2	92.7	23.8	3,473	152
Oklahoma	66.0	15.1	91.6	22.1	2,701	136
South Carolina	53.7	13.4	90.7	23.0	3,005	(NA)
Tennessee	56.2	12.6	89.6	22.7	2,842	145
Texas	62.6	16.9	93.9	25.3	3,584	139
Virginia	62.4	19.1	93.2	25.5	3,809	212
Other populous states						
Illinois	66.5	16.2	82.6	28.4	3,980	156
Indiana	66.4	12.5	87.6	25.7	3,379	138
Massachusetts	72.2	20.0	85.4	28.4	4,856	321
Michigan	68.0	14.3	92.6	31.5	3,954	139
New Jersey	67.4	18.3	81.6	28.9	6,120	237
New York	66.3	17.9	82.9	32.6	6,299	221
Ohio	67.0	13.7	86.0	26.3	3,769	149
Pennsylvania	64.7	13.6	80.1	27.4	4,752	171
United States	66.5	16.2	87.9	26.7	3,970	178

(NA) Not available.

[a] Percentage of persons age 25 and over who are high school graduates or college graduates.

[b] Public school enrollment, fall 1985, as a percentage of persons 5–17 on July 1, 1985.

[c] Average daily attendance.

[d] Based on July 1, 1985 preliminary resident population.

Source: U.S. Department of Commerce, Bureau of the Census, *Statistical Abstract of the United States, 1988.*

3. Continuing the education theme, the graph below shows percentage expenditures for education for 15 selected countries.

    a. What is the median percentage expenditure for education? Which country has this value? How does the United States compare to this median?

    b. The approximate Gross Domestic Product (total value of goods and services produced) for the 15 countries are provided (in billions of dollars) below.

Denmark	57.9	Australia	184.0
Sweden	100.0	United States	3,855.0
Canada	367.0	United Kingdom	453.0
Netherlands	122.4	Switzerland	93.7
Norway	57.0	Japan	1,300.0
France	563.0	Italy	368.0
Austria	68.8	West Germany	678.0
Belgium	77.0		

Find the approximate median amount actually spent on education in 1987. Which country has this value? Does the United States improve its position when the comparison is made on actual amounts spent? Is the latter a fair comparison?

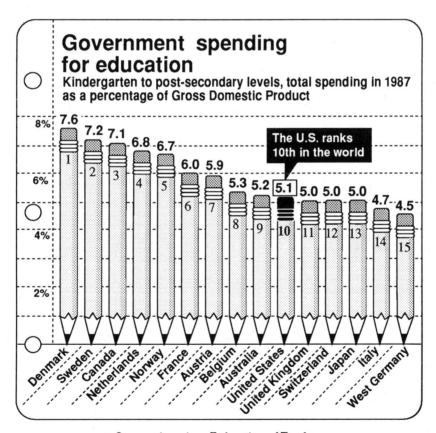

Source: American Federation of Teachers
Associated Press

4. Medians can be approximated from frequency and/or relative frequency data. The table "Age Distribution: 1900 to 2000" shows the number and percentage of people in each age class for various years. For example, the 1900 block shows that 12.1% of the U.S. population was under age 5 in that year, 22.3% was between 5 and 14, and 19.7% was between 15 and 24. The median age is that age value which 50% of the people are below and 50% are above. Since only 12.1% + 22.3% = 34.4% are under age 14, the median must be above 14. But 34.4% + 19.7% = 54.1% are age 24 or under; therefore, the median must be below 24. Thus, the median age in 1900 must be between 15 and 24 (we could say that the 15–24 group is the median age class).

   a. Approximate the median age for each year given. Comment on any differences or trends you may see.

   b. How could we improve these approximations of the median?

   c. Can you think of other ways to display these data to show the shifts in the age distributions?

Age Distribution: 1900 to 2000 (numbers in thousands)				
	1900		1920	
	Number	Percent	Number	Percent
All Ages	76,094	100.0	106,461	100.0
Under 5	9,181	12.1	11,631	10.9
5–14	16,966	22.3	22,158	20.8
15–24	14,951	19.7	18,821	17.7
25–34	12,161	16.0	17,416	16.4
35–44	9,273	12.2	14,382	13.5
45–54	6,437	8.5	10,505	9.9
55–64	4,026	5.3	6,619	6.2
65 and Over	3,099	4.1	4,929	4.6
	1940		1960	
	Number	Percent	Number	Percent
All Ages	132,122	100.0	180,671	100.0
Under 5	10,579	8.0	20,341	11.3
5–14	22,363	16.9	35,735	19.8
15–24	24,033	18.2	24,576	13.6
25–34	21,446	16.2	22,919	12.7
35–44	18,422	13.9	22,221	13.4
45–54	15,555	11.8	20,578	11.4
55–64	10,694	8.1	15,625	8.6
65 and Over	9,031	6.8	16,675	9.2

Continued on next page

Age Distribution: 1900 to 2000 (*continued*) (numbers in thousands)				
	1980		1986	
	Number	Percent	Number	Percent
All Ages	227,757	100.0	241,596	100.0
Under 5	16,485	7.2	18,128	7.5
5–14	34,845	15.3	33,855	14.0
15–24	42,743	18.8	39,261	16.3
25–34	37,626	16.5	42,984	17.8
35–44	25,868	11.4	33,142	13.7
45–54	22,754	10.0	22,823	9.4
55–64	21,761	9.6	22,230	9.2
65 and Over	25,704	11.3	29,173	12.1
	2000 (Projections)			
	Number	Percent		
All Ages	267,955	100.0		
Under 5	17,626	6.6		
5–14	38,277	14.3		
15–24	36,088	13.5		
25–34	36,415	13.6		
35–44	43,743	16.3		
45–54	37,119	13.9		
55–64	23,767	8.9		
65 and Over	34,921	13.0		

Source: *USA by Numbers*, Zero Population Growth, Inc., Washington, D.C., 1988.

Measures of Variability

Some people make decisions about where to live on the basis of weather conditions. The following table gives the monthly mean temperatures for two cities, St. Louis and San Francisco, in different parts of the United States.

Monthly Mean Temperatures (in degrees Fahrenheit)		
	St. Louis	San Francisco
January	29	49
February	34	52
March	43	53
April	56	55
May	66	58
June	75	61
July	79	62
August	75	63
September	70	64
October	58	61
November	45	55
December	34	49

Source: *World Almanac*, 1992.

If we wanted to learn generally how hot or cold it gets in these two cities, it would certainly make sense for us to calculate their mean temperatures.

	St. Louis	San Francisco
Mean Temperature	55.3	56.8
Median Temperature	57.0	56.5

Looking at this information alone, we might think that these two cities have very similar weather conditions since both have mean and median temperatures in the mid-50s. San Francisco has a slightly higher mean temperature, while St. Louis has a slightly higher median temperature.

But there is a problem with this comparison. A closer look at the data reveals that for most of the year, very different temperature conditions exist in these two cities. St. Louis has cold winters and long, hot summers, while San Francisco has very moderate winters and temperatures during the summer months that many would find very cool for that time of the year. Even though St. Louis and San Francisco have almost identical mean temperatures and almost identical median temperatures, the two cities nonetheless have very dissimilar climates. What, if any, properties of the data sets might alert us to this discrepancy?

The temperatures for San Francisco are fairly consistent throughout the year. There is little *variability* among them. However, St. Louis has some cold temperatures, some warm temperatures, and some moderate temperatures. There is a large amount of variability among them. Variability is an important aspect of this and almost any data set. Therefore, it is extremely useful for us to be able to portray and measure variability. How can we do this graphically?

We have used line plots to depict data and measures of center. Line plots can also be used to depict variability. Following are line plots of the temperature data for both St. Louis and San Francisco. These graphs indicate that there is a great deal more variability in the temperature data for St. Louis than for San Francisco. Note that in order for these comparisons of variability to be valid, both line plots must be on the same scale.

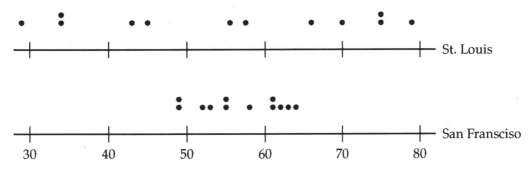

Comparative Line Plots of Monthly Temperatures (in degrees Fahrenheit)
in St. Louis and San Francisco

Another type of plot that is useful for depicting variability is a *box plot,* which uses a number line and five numbers to summarize the following set of data:

> 1. the lower extreme
> 2. the lower quartile
> 3. the median
> 4. the upper quartile
> 5. the upper extreme

The lower and upper extremes are simply the smallest and largest data elements in the set. Thus, the St. Louis extremes are as follows:

> lower extreme = 29
> upper extreme = 79

The median, or centerpoint, of the ordered data is 57. The lower quartile is the median of all the data elements less than 57, and the upper quartile is the median of all the data elements greater than 57. Thus, the St. Louis data have the following quartiles:

> lower quartile = 38.5
> upper quartile = 72.5

In a box plot, these five numbers are depicted with boxes and whiskers and are drawn above a number line as shown here:

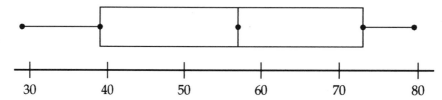

Box Plot of Monthly Temperatures (in Degrees Fahrenheit) in St. Louis

Application 5

Comparing the Variability in Two Data Sets Using Box Plots

Find the lower and upper extremes, the lower and upper quartiles, and the median for the San Francisco data and then sketch a box plot of this data set. Copy the box plot for the St. Louis data just below your San Francisco box plot, using the same scale for comparison (that is, locate both box plots above the same number line). Write a paragraph explaining the differences between the box plots. How do they show that there is more variability among the St. Louis temperatures than among the San Francisco temperatures?

To create a box plot, we have to order the data. With just 12 data elements, as in the monthly temperature data sets, this is not difficult. However, as the number of data elements to be ordered grows larger, this task can become tedious and subject to error. One technique that helps with the ordering process is the creation of a *stem-and-leaf plot*.

To create a stem-and-leaf plot for two-digit data, proceed this way: First, on the left side of a vertical line, vertically list the tens digits in order from low to high or high to low. These are the stems. For the St. Louis temperature data, the stems are shown below. The stems indicate that some of the temperatures might be from 20° F to 29° F, some from 30° F to 39° F, and so forth.

```
2 |
3 |
4 |
5 |
6 |
7 |
```

Next, write down the units digit for each data element on the right of the vertical line in the row corresponding to its tens digit. These are the leaves. For the St. Louis temperature data, we get the following:

```
2 | 9
3 | 4 4
4 | 3 5
5 | 6 8
6 | 6
7 | 5 9 5 0
```

Finally, order the leaves on each individual stem as shown below. In the above plot, only the leaves on the 70s stem are out of order and need reordering.

```
2 | 9
3 | 4 4
4 | 3 5
5 | 6 8
6 | 6
7 | 0 5 5 9
```
Key: 2 | 9 = 29 degrees Fahrenheit

The 2 and the 9 on the top line represent 29. The 3 and the two 4s on the second line represent two 34s, and so on. The *key* tells what a typical stem and leaf represents. The data are now ordered. Later we shall explore other uses for the stem-and-leaf plot.

Application 6

Creating a Stem-and-Leaf Plot

Create a stem-and-leaf plot for the San Francisco temperature data. How does it differ from the stem-and-leaf plot for the St. Louis temperature data?

The line plot and box plot are good ways to *show* variability. Let's look at some ways we can *measure* variability. After calculating these measures, we can examine how well they match with the visual images of variability created by a line plot or a box plot.

By far the simplest measure of variability is the *range*. The range is the largest element in the data set minus the smallest. For example, the ranges for our sets of temperature data are as follows:

St. Louis	50
San Francisco	15

Note that the larger range for the St. Louis data agrees with the impression created by the line plot shown on p. 23. Because the range uses only the largest and smallest elements in a data set, it tells us nothing about the variability of all the data elements between the extremes. There are at least three other measures of variability that are usually preferable to the range because each more accurately describes the variability throughout an entire data set than does the range.

One of these measures is the *interquartile range (IQR)*, or the upper quartile minus the lower quartile. In other words, it is the width of the box in a box plot. The interquartile range is only slightly more difficult to compute than the range, and it is far more stable if the data set contains one or more outliers—that is, data that are significantly larger or smaller than the rest. The *IQRs* for our sets of temperature data are the following:

St. Louis   34.0
San Francisco 9.0

Again, St. Louis has the larger variability.

A natural measure of variability is the *mean deviation*. The mean deviation is the average of the distances between each data element and the mean of all of the data (that is, the average of the absolute values of the differences between each datum and the mean of all the data). A set of data with elements that cluster very closely about the mean, as seen in the line plot for the San Francisco temperatures, has a small mean deviation and little variability, while a set of data like the one for St. Louis temperatures has a large mean deviation and much variability.

Here is how to compute the mean deviation using the St. Louis temperature data. The mean monthly temperature for St. Louis is 55.3 degrees. The January temperature is 29. The distance between these two numbers is $|29 - 55.3| = 26.3$. Similarly, the distance between the February temperature, 34 degrees, and the mean is $|34 - 55.3| = 21.3$. The mean of these absolute values for all 12 months is the mean deviation.

Follow these steps to calculate a mean deviation:

1. Find the mean of all the data (add up all the data elements and divide by how many there are).

2. Find the difference between each data element and the mean.

3. Take the absolute value of each of these differences.

4. Find the mean of the absolute values.

The following chart shows how to calculate the mean deviation using the St. Louis temperature data.

Calculating a Mean Deviation				
Month	Datum	Mean	Datum – Mean	|Datum –Mean|
January	29	55.3	–26.3	26.3
February	34	55.3	–21.3	21.3
March	43	55.3	–12.3	12.3
April	56	55.3	0.7	0.7
May	66	55.3	10.7	10.7
June	75	55.3	19.7	19.7
July	79	55.3	23.7	23.7
August	75	55.3	19.7	19.7
September	70	55.3	14.7	14.7
October	58	55.3	2.7	2.7
November	45	55.3	–10.3	10.3
December	34	55.3	–21.3	21.3

The mean of the \|Datum – Mean\| column, 15.3, is the mean deviation.

Application 7

Calculating a Mean Deviation

Calculate the mean deviation for the San Francisco temperature data on page 22. Write a few sentences explaining why it differs from the mean deviation for the St. Louis temperature data.

Another common measure of variability is the *standard deviation*, which is very similar to the mean deviation. The major difference in computing the two is that the standard deviation squares the difference between each data element and the mean—instead of taking the absolute value—to remove any negative signs from the differences (the advantage of this is rooted in statistical theory). To compensate for this squaring, the square root is taken at the end.

Follow these steps to calculate a standard deviation:

1. Find the mean of all the data.

2. Find the difference between each data element and the mean.

3. Square each of the differences.

4. Find the mean of the squares (sum the squares and divide by the number of data elements).

5. Take the square root of the mean of the squares.

The following chart shows how to calculate the standard deviation using the St. Louis temperature data.

Calculating a Standard Deviation				
Month	Data	Mean	Datum – Mean	$(Datum - Mean)^2$
January	29	55.3	−26.3	691.7
February	34	55.3	−21.3	453.7
March	43	55.3	−12.3	151.3
April	56	55.3	0.7	0.5
May	66	55.3	10.7	114.5
June	75	55.3	19.7	388.1
July	79	55.3	23.7	561.7
August	75	55.3	19.7	388.1
September	70	55.3	14.7	216.1
October	58	55.3	2.7	7.3
November	45	55.3	−10.3	106.1
December	34	55.3	−21.3	453.7

The mean of the numbers in the $(Datum - Mean)^2$ column is 294.4. The square root of this number, 17.2, is the standard deviation.

Application 8

Calculating a Standard Deviation

Calculate the standard deviation of the monthly temperature data for San Francisco. Write a few sentences telling why it differs from the standard deviation of the St. Louis temperature data.

Although the mean deviation and the standard deviation are complex quantities, they reflect a measure of the typical distance that data elements vary from the mean. For the St. Louis temperatures, these two measures of variability are 15.3 and 17.2. Looking at the chart on page 27 in the |Data – Mean| column (the amount each data element varies from the mean), you will see that indeed many distances are close to these numbers. By looking at your calculations in either Application 7 or Application 8, you will see that the distances between data elements and the mean are close to these numbers for the San Francisco data, too.

Notice that the four measures of variability just discussed all tell the same story numerically that the line plots and box plots told pictorially. Notice also that calculating the standard deviation can be tedious, even using a calculator. Fortunately, because the standard deviation is frequently used to describe the variability in data sets, many calculators have a standard deviation key. The symbol on this key may be the lowercase Greek letter sigma (σ). If you have this key, you also have a key for obtaining a mean—and you are but two keystrokes away from having both the standard deviation and the mean after having entered your data a single time.

In summary, a small measure of variability tells us that most of the data points are clustered close to the center of the data set. A large measure of variability warns us to examine the data carefully to determine whether the mean or median is the best measure of the center. Also, by computing the same measure of variability for each of two or more data sets, a great deal can be learned about the relative consistency of the data sets.

Exploring Measures of Center and Variability

1. The data below show the number of base hits by American League and National League baseball teams during the 1991 season.

   a. Which league was the better-hitting league? Justify your answer.

   b. Which league exhibited the most variability among its teams? Justify your answer.

American	Hits	National	Hits
Baltimore	1421	Atlanta	1407
Boston	1486	Chicago	1395
California	1396	Cincinnati	1419
Chicago	1464	Houston	1345
Cleveland	1390	Los Angeles	1366
Detroit	1372	Montreal	1329
Kansas City	1475	New York	1305
Milwaukee	1523	Philadelphia	1332
Minnesota	1557	Pittsburgh	1433
New York	1418	St. Louis	1366
Oakland	1342	San Diego	1321
Seattle	1400	San Francisco	1345
Texas	1539		
Toronto	1412		

Source: *Peterson's Pro Baseball 1992.*

2. The following lists give the prices (rounded to the nearest dollar) of books that were best-sellers during a particular week. For each category, fiction and nonfiction, do the following:

   a. Calculate the mean.

   b. Calculate the median.

   c. Calculate the range.

   d. Calculate the interquartile range.

   e. Calculate the mean deviation.

   f. Calculate the standard deviation.

   g. Draw a line plot of the data.

   h. Draw a box plot of the data.

Then write several sentences describing what these numbers and plots tell—or don't tell—about the two sets of data.

Fiction	
1. *The Sands of Time,* by Sidney Sheldon	$20
2. *The Cardinal of the Kremlin,* by Tom Clancy	$20
3. *Alaska,* by James Michener	$23
4. *The Polar Express,* by Chris Van Allsburg	$17
5. *One,* by Richard Bach	$18
6. *Dear Mili,* by Wilhelm Grimm	$17
7. *The Queen of the Damned,* by Anne Rice	$19
8. *Anything for Billy,* by Larry McMurtry	$19
9. *Final Flight,* by Stephen Coots	$19
10. *Mitla Pass,* by Leon Uris	$20
11. *Breathing Lessons,* by Anne Tyler	$19
12. *Spy Hook,* by Anne Tyler	$19
13. *Zoya,* by Danielle Steel	$20
14. *The Shell Seekers,* by Rosamunde Pilcher	$20
15. *Love in the Time of Cholera,* by Gabriel Garcia Marquez	$19

Nonfiction	
1. *All I Need to Know I Learned in Kindergarten,* by Robert Fulghum	$16
2. *Gracie,* by George Burns	$17
3. *A Brief History of Time,* by Stephen W. Hawking	$19
4. *Child Star,* by Shirley Temple Black	$20
5. *Seven Stories of Christmas Love,* by Leo Buscalia	$13
6. *The Last Lion,* by William Manchester	$25
7. *Don't Bend Over in the Garden, Granny, You Know Them Taters Got Eyes,* by Lewis Grizzard	$16
8. *Christmas in America,* edited by David Cohen	$35
9. *A Bright Shining Lie,* by Neil Sheehan	$25
10. *Chronicle of the 20th Century,* edited by Clifton Daniel	$50
11. *Talking Straight,* by Lee Iacocca	$22
12. *The Home Planet,* edited by Kevin W. Kelley	$40
13. *Goldwater,* by Barry M. Goldwater	$22
14. *The First Salute,* by Barbara W. Tuchman	$23
15. *Press On!* by Chuck Yeager	$18

Source: *New York Times Book Review,* January 1, 1989.

3. Until very recently, Kuwait (as described in Application 2) was a country where only a few families had a great deal of wealth and most of the people had very little money. The per-capita income (mean income) for Kuwait has long been among the highest in the world, exceeding that of the United States. The United

States, while having its share of both very wealthy and very poor, differs from Kuwait in that it is dominated by a large middle class.

a. Which nation do you believe would have the higher median income? Explain.

b. Which nation do you believe would have a higher mean income? Explain.

4. As in many cities, housing prices in Madison, Wisconsin, vary from one part of town to another. The lists below give the prices of houses advertised by a single real estate agent on the east and west sides of town. Use the mean, median, range, interquartile range, mean deviation, standard deviation, line plots, and box plots to analyze these data. In particular, try to answer these questions:

a. On which side of town is the available housing more expensive?

b. On which side of town is the price of available housing more variable? Why?

c. How well do the mean and median describe the price of houses in each part of town?

Price of Houses on the East and West Sides of Madison, Wisconsin (rounded to nearest thousand dollars)
West Side:
80, 123, 72, 90, 39, 90, 81, 82, 79, 110, 80, 290, 80, 180, 38, 105, 165, 80, 90, 80, 30, 80, 75, 90, 50, 72, 165, 70, 68, 85, 80, 68, 108, 128, 110, 76, 80, 62.
East Side:
45, 75, 83, 90, 58, 30, 42, 81, 80, 79, 58, 57, 73, 65, 75, 67, 62, 70, 104, 98, 86, 55, 42, 45, 46, 47, 72, 39, 37, 75, 70, 60, 94, 90, 40, 79, 55, 60, 55, 78, 27.

Source: *In Business*, January 1989.

Uses of the Mean and Standard Deviation

The mean and the standard deviation are frequently used to make different sets of data more comparable. For example, consider the national average SAT and ACT mathematics scores for the years 1970–89.

Year	SAT	ACT
1970	488	20.0
1971	488	19.1
1972	484	18.8
1973	481	19.1
1974	480	18.3
1975	472	17.6
1976	472	17.5
1977	470	17.4
1978	468	17.5
1979	467	17.5
1980	466	17.4
1981	466	17.3
1982	467	17.2
1983	468	16.9
1984	471	17.3
1985	475	17.2
1986	475	17.3
1987	476	17.2
1988	476	17.2
1989	476	17.2

Source: *The Condition of Education, 1991*, U. S. Department of Education

The scores on these two tests are not directly comparable because they are measured on different scales and have vastly different means and standard deviations.

	SAT	ACT
mean	474.30	17.75
standard deviation	6.78	0.82

One way to make these two data sets more comparable is to center them by subtracting the mean SAT score, 474.3, from each SAT score and by subtracting the mean ACT score, 17.75, from each ACT score. Line plots of the resulting sets of centered data follow. It may be seen that the transformed data are centered at zero but are still not comparable because their standard deviations are so different.

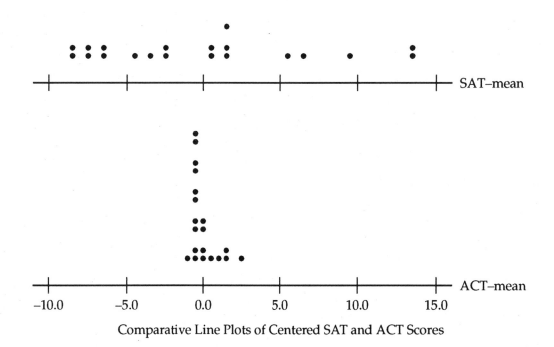

Comparative Line Plots of Centered SAT and ACT Scores

By dividing each centered SAT score by the standard deviation of all the SAT scores, 6.78, and by dividing each centered ACT score by the standard deviation of all of the ACT scores, 0.82, two new sets of *standardized* scores are obtained, as in columns 4 and 7 of the next table.

Calculating Standardized SAT and ACT Scores						
Year	SAT	SAT – mean	$\dfrac{\text{SAT – mean}}{\text{st. dev.}}$	ACT	ACT – mean	$\dfrac{\text{ACT – mean}}{\text{st. dev.}}$
1970	488	13.7000	2.02065	20.0	2.25000	2.74390
1971	488	13.7000	2.02065	19.1	1.35000	1.64634
1972	484	9.7000	1.43068	18.8	1.05000	1.28049
1973	481	6.7000	0.98820	19.1	1.35000	1.64634
1974	480	5.7000	0.84071	18.3	0.55000	0.67073
1975	472	–2.3000	–0.33923	17.6	–0.15000	–0.18293
1976	472	–2.3000	–0.33923	17.5	–0.25000	–0.30488
1977	470	–4.3000	–0.63422	17.4	–0.35000	–0.42683
1978	468	–6.3000	–0.92920	17.5	–0.25000	–0.30488
1979	467	–7.3000	–1.07669	17.5	–0.25000	–0.30488
1980	466	–8.3000	–1.22419	17.4	–0.35000	–0.42683
1981	466	–8.3000	–1.22419	17.3	–0.45000	–0.54878
1982	467	–7.3000	–1.07669	17.2	–0.55000	–0.67073
1983	468	–6.3000	–0.92920	16.9	–0.85000	–1.03659
1984	471	–3.3000	–0.48672	17.3	–0.45000	–0.54878
1985	475	0.7000	0.10325	17.2	–0.55000	–0.67073
1986	475	0.7000	0.10325	17.3	–0.45000	–0.54878
1987	476	1.7000	0.25074	17.2	–0.55000	–0.67073
1988	476	1.7000	0.25074	17.2	–0.55000	–0.67073
1989	476	1.7000	0.25074	17.2	–0.55000	–0.67073

Comparative line plots of the standardized SAT scores, labeled S-STAND, and the standardized ACT scores, labeled A-STAND, indicate the two sets of standardized data are comparable. How would you describe these sets of standardized scores?

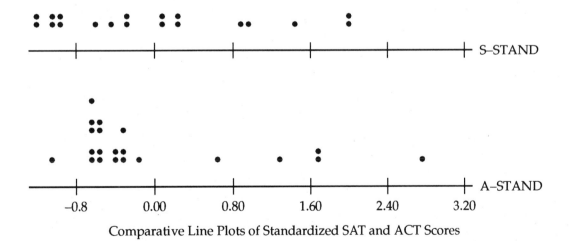

Comparative Line Plots of Standardized SAT and ACT Scores

Additionally, because the SAT and ACT scores were collected from year to year, trends in each variable can be observed by plotting the ordered pairs

(year, standardized SAT score) and (year, standardized ACT score)

on separate Cartesian planes. Each plot is called a *time-series plot*. To make it easier to compare patterns over time, the two time-series plots can be superimposed to create a single plot like the one below. In this plot, each *A* represents an ordered pair of the form (year, standardized ACT score) and each *B* represents an ordered pair of the form (year, standardized SAT score). For example, the top left *B* indicates the point (1970, 2.02065) and the *A* above it indicates the point (1970, 2.74390). Describe the patterns you see in these trends over time.

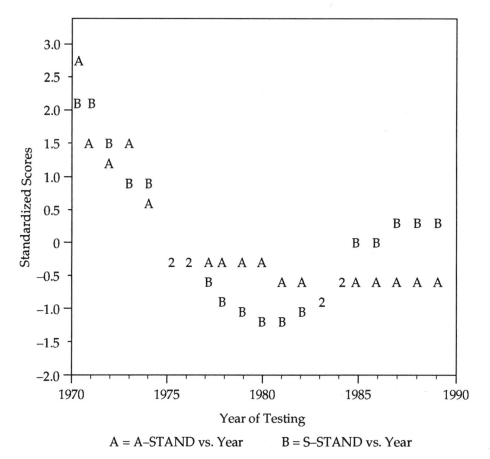

A = A–STAND vs. Year   B = S–STAND vs. Year

Scatter Plot of Standardized ACT and SAT Scores Over Time
("2" indicates two points at or near this location)

Using the standardized scores, it is possible to determine, for example, what ACT score would be comparable to a 470 on the SAT. To do this, let *X* be the unknown ACT score and set the standardized SAT and ACT scores equal to each other as follows:

$$\frac{470-474.3}{6.78} = \frac{X-17.75}{0.82}$$

By solving this equation for *X*, we find that a score of 17.23 on the ACT test is comparable to a score of 470 on the SAT test.

Playing Around

The following table gives the number of minutes played and the number of field goals attempted (FGA) by the Minnesota Timberwolves during the 1991–92 season through March 1, 1992.

Player	Minutes	FGA
Campbell	1817	844
Richardson	1976	831
West	1679	593
Mitchell	1617	530
Glass	1098	535
Bailey	1359	504
Spencer	874	203
Breuer	1012	291
Brooks	764	247
Garrick	486	126
Longley	577	138
Randall	241	80
Murphy	301	46

Source: *USA Today*, March 3, 1992.

1. Are the two sets of data comparable? Explain.

2. For each player, transform the number of minutes played and the number of field goals attempted into standardized scores.

3. Draw separate line plots for each set of standardized scores. What do you observe?

4. If a Timberwolf attempted 600 field goals, approximately how many minutes would you expect him to have played?

5. If a Timberwolf played 1200 minutes, approximately how many field goals would you expect him to have attempted?

Danger on Mt. McKinley

As the table below indicates, during each year from 1980 to 1991 only about one-half the hundreds of climbers who attempted to reach the summit of Mt. McKinley (North America's highest and coldest mountain) made it.

Year	Number of Climbers	Number Successful
1980	659	283
1981	612	321
1982	696	310
1983	709	474
1984	695	324
1985	645	321
1986	755	406
1987	817	251
1988	916	551
1989	1009	517
1990	998	573
1991	935	553

Source: *USA Today*, June 29, 1992.

1. Are the two sets of data comparable? Explain.

2. For each year, transform the number of climbers and the number of successful climbers into standardized scores.

3. Are the two sets of standardized scores comparable? Explain.

4. How many people would you expect to reach the summit of Mt. McKinley if 800 attempted the climb this year?

5. Draw a single time-series plot of the two sets of standardized scores. From this plot determine if there are any trends in the original data.

The mean and the standard deviation are also frequently used to identify unusually large or small numbers in a data set. A data point that is two or more standard deviations away from the mean—either below or above it— is considered unusual. If the standardized data point is 2 or greater, or −2 or less, then that datum is more than two standard deviations away from the mean. (Remember that the standardized data point is equal to $\dfrac{\text{datum} - \text{mean}}{\text{st. dev.}}$.) For example, consider the total player costs (in millions of dollars) for each of the 27 teams in the National Basketball Association (NBA) during the 1990–91 season. The mean and standard deviation of these data are $12.26 and $1.62 million, respectively.

Team	Player Costs
L.A. Lakers	$13.0
Detroit Pistons	14.1
Boston Celtics	14.5
Chicago Bulls	10.8
N.Y. Knicks	14.8
Cleveland Cavaliers	15.6
Phoenix Suns	12.4
Portland Trail Blazers	12.4
Charlotte Hornets	11.4
Sacramento Kings	11.9
Philadelphia 76ers	13.4
Golden State Warriors	12.7
San Antonio Spurs	12.7
Orlando Magic	8.5
NM Timberwolves	8.7
Houston Rockets	12.9
Dallas Mavericks	12.7
Miami Heat	9.6
Atlanta Hawks	12.9
Milwaukee Bucks	12.7
New Jersey Nets	12.8

Continued on next page

Team	Player Costs
	continued
L.A. Clippers	11.5
Utah Jazz	12.1
Denver Nuggets	12.4
Washington Bullets	10.4
Seattle SuperSonics	11.8
Indiana Pacers	12.2

Source: *USA Today*, June 16, 1992.

How many standard deviations away from the mean are the player costs for the Cleveland Cavaliers, the Orlando Magic, and the Minnesota Timberwolves? Do the player costs for these teams deviate enough from the mean to be considered unusual? Do any other teams have unusually high or low player costs? To answer the questions, look at the following:

Cleveland Cavaliers: $\dfrac{15.6-12.26}{1.62} = 2.06 \geq 2$

Orlando Magic $\dfrac{8.5-12.26}{1.62} = -2.32 \leq -2$

MN Timberwolves: $\dfrac{8.7-12.26}{1.62} = -2.20 \leq -2$

The \$15.6 million player costs of the Cleveland Cavaliers are 2.06 standard deviations above the mean, and the player costs of the Orlando Magic and the Minnesota Timberwolves are 2.32 and 2.20 standard deviations below the mean. Consequently, the player costs for all three teams are considered unusual. Similar calculations show that none of the other NBA teams have unusual player costs. Alternately, we could have arrived at these same conclusions by noting the following:

$$15.6 \geq 12.26 + 2(1.62)$$

$$8.5 \leq 12.26 - 2(1.62)$$

$$8.7 \leq 12.26 - 2(1.62)$$

Here is the reason the two sets of computations yield the same results:

$$\text{datum} \geq \text{mean} + 2(\text{standard deviation})$$

if and only if

$$\frac{\text{datum} - \text{mean}}{\text{standard deviation}} \geq 2$$

and

$$\text{datum} \leq \text{mean} - 2(\text{standard deviation})$$

if and only if

$$\frac{\text{datum} - \text{mean}}{\text{standard deviation}} \leq -2$$

The easy way to use these criteria to identify unusually large or small numbers in a data set is to first compute the mean and the standard deviation of all the data and then apply either of the formulas only to the largest and smallest numbers in the set of data. Whichever formula you use, be advised of the following:

1. Many data sets will have no unusually large or small numbers.

2. Some data sets will only have unusually large numbers, and some data sets will only have unusually small numbers.

3. Some data sets will have both unusually large and unusually small numbers.

4. Very few numbers in a data set will ever be declared unusually large or small.

Data that are unusually large or small are sometimes called *outliers*. A box plot may also be used to identify outliers. By this method, any datum that is more than 1.5 times the *interquartile range (IQR)* below the *lower quartile (LQ)* or above the *upper quartile (UQ)* is called an outlier. (Recall that the upper quartile is the median of the "upper half" of the data, the lower quartile is the median of the "lower half" of the data, and the interquartile range is the upper quartile minus the lower quartile.)

For example, the lower and upper quartiles for the player costs for each of the 27 NBA teams during the 1990–91 season are $11.5 and $12.9 million, respectively. Thus, the $IQR = 12.9 - 11.5 = 1.4$, and a particular team's player costs is called an outlier if it is less than $LQ - 1.5(IQR) = 11.5 - 1.5(1.4) = 9.4$ or larger than $UQ + 1.5(IQR) = 12.9 + 1.5(1.4) = 15.0$. In this example, the box plot method and the MEAN ± 2(STANDARD DEVIATION) method both classify exactly the same set of data as outliers. Generally, this does not happen because it is usually much more difficult for a datum to be outside the interval

$$(LQ - 1.5(IQR), UQ + 1.5(IQR))$$

than to be outside

$$(\text{MEAN} - 2(\text{STANDARD DEVIATION}), \text{MEAN} + 2(\text{STANDARD DEVIATION})).$$

An outlier by the box plot method is likely to be an outlier by the MEAN ± 2(STAN-DARD DEVIATION) method, but an outlier by the MEAN ± 2(STANDARD DEVIA-TION) method may not be an outlier by the box-plot method.

Application 12

Wow, That's Unusual!

Listed below are the franchise values and the total revenues (in millions of dollars) for each of the 27 teams in the National Basketball Association (NBA) during the 1990–91 season.

Team	Franchise Value	Total Revenue
L.A. Lakers	$150	62.6
Detroit Pistons	120	45.0
Boston Celtics	110	41.8
Chicago Bulls	100	41.2
New York Knicks	83	33.8
Cleveland Cavaliers	81	35.3
Phoenix Suns	80	29.9
Portland Trail Blazers	78	36.2
Charlotte Hornets	74	34.4
Sacramento Kings	63	26.3
Philadelphia 76ers	63	30.1
Golden State Warriors	63	30.8
San Antonio Spurs	63	33.0
Orlando Magic	62	27.3
Minnesota Timberwolves	62	32.7
Houston Rockets	61	28.4
Dallas Mavericks	60	29.3
Miami Heat	60	26.3
Atlanta Hawks	57	24.7
Milwaukee Bucks	56	24.2
New Jersey Nets	54	26.8
L.A. Clippers	54	28.3
Utah Jazz	52	27.5
Denver Nuggets	46	21.5
Washington Bullets	46	21.6
Seattle Supersonics	45	22.4
Indiana Pacers	43	21.7

Source: *USA Today*, June 16, 1992.

1. Are any of the total revenues outliers using the MEAN ± 2(STANDARD DEVIA-TION) method? If so, how many standard deviations away from the mean are they and what might be the reasons for a team to have unusually large or small total revenue?

2. Are any of the total revenues outliers by the box-plot method?

3. Do the two methods identify the same outliers for the total revenue data?

4. Are any of the franchise values outliers using the MEAN ± 2(STANDARD DEVI-ATION) method? If so, how many standard deviations away from the mean are they and what might cause the corresponding teams to have unusually large or small franchise values?

5. Are any of the franchise values outliers by the box-plot method?

6. Do the two methods identify the same outliers for the franchise value data?

The 1991 per-capita income (total income of all residents divided by the number of residents) for each of the 50 states and the District of Columbia is listed below.

State	Per-capita Income[a]	State	Per-capita Income[a]
Alabama	$15,367	Montana	$16,043
Alaska	21,932	Nebraska	17,852
Arizona	16,401	Nevada	19,175
Arkansas	14,733	New Hampshire	20,951
California	20,592	New Jersey	25,372
Colorado	19,440	New Mexico	14,844
Connecticut	25,881	New York	22,456
Delaware	20,349	North Carolina	16,642
District of Columbia	24,439	North Dakota	16,088
Florida	18,880	Ohio	17,916
Georgia	17,364	Oklahoma	15,827
Hawaii	21,306	Oregon	17,592
Idaho	15,401	Pennsylvania	19,128
Illinois	20,824	Rhode Island	18,840
Indiana	17,217	South Carolina	15,420
Iowa	17,505	South Dakota	16,392
Kansas	18,511	Tennessee	16,325
Kentucky	15,539	Texas	17,305
Louisiana	15,143	Utah	14,529
Maine	17,306	Vermont	17,747
Maryland	22,080	Virginia	19,976
Massachusetts	22,987	Washington	19,442
Michigan	18,679	West Virginia	14,174
Minnesota	19,107	Wisconsin	18,046
Mississippi	13,343	Wyoming	17,118
Missouri	17,842		

*rounded to the nearest dollar

Source: *MEA Today*, October 1992.

7. Verify that the mean and standard deviation of the per-capita incomes for the 50 states and the District of Columbia are $18,301 and $2,846, respectively, when rounded to the nearest dollar.

8. Are any of the per-capita incomes outliers by the MEAN ± 2(STANDARD DEVIATION) method? By the box-plot method? Do the two methods produce the same results? What might cause a region to have an unusually high per-capita income? An unusually low per-capita income?

9. Do you think the mean of the per-capita incomes for the 50 states and the District of Columbia ($18,301) equals the per-capita income for the United States? Why or why not?

10. Class Activity: Find some data in newspapers, magazines, or books which contain outliers by either of the methods described. Is it difficult to find such data? Do most data sets contain outliers?

11. Using the MEAN ± 2(STANDARD DEVIATION) criteria, find (or make up!) a set of the following:

   a. Five numbers that contains one outlier.

   b. Eight numbers containing two outliers, one small and the other large.

When data are accumulated over time, values that fall outside the interval MEAN ± 2(STANDARD DEVIATION) are sometimes said to be "out of control." A standard graphical technique for identifying points that are out of control involves the construction of a scatter plot, called a *control chart*, whose horizontal axis represents the time when the data were observed, with two horizontal lines, one passing through the point (0, MEAN – 2(STANDARD DEVIATION)) and the other passing through (0, MEAN + 2(STANDARD DEVIATION)). Points below the lower horizontal line or above the upper horizontal line are those that are out of control. In a manufacturing process, these points are given special attention to see if the entire process has gone out of control or if rare events have been observed.

Below are the batting averages of the American League batting champions from 1941 through 1991 and a control chart for these data. The mean and standard deviation for the data are .343 and .021, respectively, so that the horizontal lines on the control chart pass through the points (1941, .343 – 2(.021)) = (1941, .301) and (1941, .343 + 2(.021)) = (1941, .385). For ease of interpretation, the points on the graph are labeled by the last digit of the year in which the batting average was recorded. Notice that four batting averages are identified as being out of control: Ted Williams's .406 and .388 in 1941 and 1957, respectively; Rod Carew's .388 in 1977; and George Brett's .390 in 1980. It may be shown that only Ted Williams's .406 in 1941 is identified as an outlier by the box-plot method.

Batting Averages of American League Batting Champions		
Year	Player and Club	Average
1941	Theodore Williams, Boston	.406
1942	Theodore Williams, Boston	.356
1943	Lucius Appling, Chicago	.328
1944	Louis Boudreau, Cleveland	.327
1945	George Stirnweiss, New York	.309
1946	Mickey Vernon, Washington	.353
1947	Theodore Williams, Boston	.343
1948	Theodore Williams, Boston	.369
1949	George Kell, Detroit	.343
1950	William Goodman, Boston	.354
1951	Ferris Fain, Philadelphia	.344
1952	Ferris Fain, Philadelphia	.327
1953	Mickey Vernon, Washington	.337
1954	Roberto Avila, Cleveland	.341
1955	Albert Kaline, Detroit	.340
1956	Mickey Mantle, New York	.353
1957	Theodore Williams, Boston	.388
1958	Theodore Williams, Boston	.328
1959	Harvey Kuenn, Detroit	.353
1960	Pete Runnels, Boston	.320

Continued on next page

Batting Averages of American League Batting Champions		
Year	Player and Club *continued*	Average
1961	Norman Cash, Detroit	.361
1962	Pete Runnels, Boston	.326
1963	Carl Yastrzemski, Boston	.321
1964	Tony Oliva, Minnesota	.323
1965	Tony Oliva, Minnesota	.321
1966	Frank Robinson, Baltimore	.316
1967	Carl Yastrzemski, Boston	.326
1968	Carl Yastrzemski, Boston	.301
1969	Rodney Carew, Minnesota	.332
1970	Alexander Johnson, California	.329
1971	Tony Oliva, Minnesota	.337
1972	Rodney Carew, Minnesota	.318
1973	Rodney Carew, Minnesota	.350
1974	Rodney Carew, Minnesota	.364
1975	Rodney Carew, Minnesota	.359
1976	George Brett, Kansas City	.333
1977	Rodney Carew, Minnesota	.388
1978	Rodney Carew, Minnesota	.333
1979	Fredric Lynn, Boston	.333
1980	George Brett, Kansas City	.390
1981	Carney Lansford, Boston	.336
1982	Willie Wilson, Kansas City	.332
1983	Wade Boggs, Boston	.361
1984	Donald Mattingly, New York	.343
1985	Wade Boggs, Boston	.368
1986	Wade Boggs, Boston	.357
1987	Wade Boggs, Boston	.363
1988	Wade Boggs, Boston	.366
1989	Kirby Puckett, Minnesota	.339
1990	George Brett, Kansas City	.329
1991	Julio Franco, Texas	.341

Source: *The Complete Baseball Record Book 1992.*

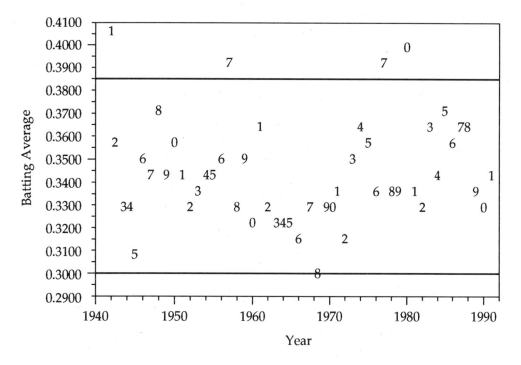

Control Chart for the Batting Averages of American League Batting Champions
(1941–91)

Application 13

Batting Averages of National League Batting Champions 1941-91

Listed below are the batting averages of the National League batting champions from 1941 through 1991.

Batting Averages of National League Batting Champions		
Year	Player and Club	Average
1941	Pete Reiser, Brooklyn	.343
1942	Ernest Lombardi, Boston	.330
1943	Stanley Musial, St. Louis	.357
1944	Fred Walker, Brooklyn	.357
1945	Phillip Cavarretta, Chicago	.355
1946	Stanley Musial, St. Louis	.365
1947	Harry Walker, St. Louis/Phil.	.363

Continued on next page

Batting Averages of National League Batting Champions		
Year	Player and Club *continued*	Average
1948	Stanley Musial, St. Louis	.376
1949	Jack Robinson, Brooklyn	.342
1950	Stanley Musial, St. Louis	.346
1951	Stanley Musial, St. Louis	.355
1952	Stanley Musial, St. Louis	.336
1953	Carl Furillo, Brooklyn	.344
1954	Willie Mays, New York	.345
1955	Richie Ashburn, Philadelphia	.338
1956	Henry Aaron, Milwaukee	.328
1957	Stanley Musial, St. Louis	.351
1958	Richie Ashburn, Philadelphia	.350
1959	Henry Aaron, Milwaukee	.355
1960	Richard Groat, Pittsburgh	.325
1961	Roberto Clemente, Pittsburgh	.351
1962	H. Thomas Davis, Los Angeles	.346
1963	H. Thomas Davis, Los Angeles	.326
1964	Roberto Clemente, Pittsburgh	.339
1965	Roberto Clemente, Pittsburgh	.329
1966	Mateo Alou, Pittsburgh	.342
1967	Roberto Clemente, Pittsburgh	.357
1968	Peter Rose, Cincinnati	.335
1969	Peter Rose, Cincinnati	.348
1970	Ricardo Carty, Atlanta	.366
1971	Joseph Torre, St. Louis	.363
1972	Billy Williams, Chicago	.333
1973	Peter Rose, Cincinnati	.338
1974	Ralph Garr, Atlanta	.353
1975	Bill Madlock, Chicago	.354
1976	Bill Madlock, Chicago	.339
1977	David Parker, Pittsburgh	.338
1978	David Parker, Pittsburgh	.334
1979	Keith Hernandez, St. Louis	.344
1980	William Buckner, Chicago	.324
1981	Bill Madlock, Pittsburgh	.341
1982	Albert Oliver, Montreal	.331
1983	Bill Madlock, Pittsburgh	.323
1984	Anthony Gwynn, San Diego	.351
1985	Willie McGee, St. Louis	.353
1986	Timothy Raines, Montreal	.334
1987	Anthony Gwynn, San Diego	.370
1988	Anthony Gwynn, San Diego	.313

Continued on next page

Batting Averages of National League Batting Champions		
Year	Player and Club *continued*	Average
1989	Anthony Gwynn, San Diego	.336
1990	Willie McGee, St. Louis	.335
1991	Terry Pendleton, Atlanta	.319

Source: *The Complete Baseball Record Book 1992.*

1. Verify that the mean and standard deviation for these data are .344 and .014, respectively, when rounded to the nearest thousandth.

2. Construct a control chart for these data. Are any of the data out of control? If so, which one(s)?

3. Are any of the data outliers by the box-plot method of outlier detection? If so, which one(s)?

4. Do the control-chart and box-plot methods identify the same data as being unusual? Why?

5. Do you think that the mean of the batting averages (.344) equals the combined batting average of all the National League batting champions from 1941–91 using only the years in which they were champions? Why or why not?

Hurricane Deaths Decline

Listed below is the number of deaths attributed to hurricanes in the United States by decade (beginning in 1900).

Year	Hurricane-related Deaths
1900–09	8100
1910–19	1050
1920–29	2130
1930–39	1050
1940–49	220
1950–59	750
1960–69	570
1970–79	226
1980–89	161

Source: *USA Today*, September 3, 1992.

1. Construct a control chart for these data. Are any of the data out of control? If so, which one(s)?

2. Does the box-plot method of detecting outliers classify any of the data as outliers? If so, which one(s)?

3. Do the control-chart and box-plot methods identify the same data as being unusual? Why?

Center and Variability—Summary

The mean and median are the two numbers used most often to locate the center of a set of data. When a line plot of the data is perfectly symmetrical, the mean and median are equal; when a line plot of the data is roughly mound-shaped, the mean and median are approximately equal; and when a line plot of the data indicates the presence of some unusually large (or small) data, the mean and median will be substantially different. In the first two cases, the mean is frequently (but not always!) used to locate the center of the data. In the last case, the median is used because it is always in the middle; and the mean will be pulled away from the middle in the direction of the unusually large (or small) number(s).

The variability in a set of data can be displayed using a line plot, a box plot, or a stem-and-leaf plot. These allow you to inspect the variability in a single set of data and to compare the variability in two or more sets of data. Frequently, variability is described by a summary number such as the range, the interquartile range (*IQR*), the absolute mean deviation, or the standard deviation. The range—which is the largest element in the set of data minus the smallest—is easy to compute. Its disadvantage is that unusually large (or small) numbers cause its value to be inflated. The *IQR*—which is the upper quartile minus the lower quartile—is only slightly more difficult to compute and is far less affected by unusually large (or small) data. The absolute mean deviation and the standard deviation are very similar numerical measures of variability, and both can be inappropriately inflated by the presence of unusually large or small data. Of all of these numerical measures of variability the one most often used is the standard deviation: although not easy to compute by hand, many calculators give its value with a single key-stroke after the data have been entered.

The two main uses of the mean and standard deviation are to make different sets of data more comparable and to identify unusually large or small numbers in a set of data. By subtracting the mean from each datum and dividing each of these differences by the standard deviation, standardized scores (data) are obtained. The standardized scores from two or more sets of data are comparable, in the sense that they are centered around zero and exhibit variability measured on similar scales. Standardized scores are frequently used to detect outliers. If a standardized score is less than or equal to –2 or greater than or equal to 2, the datum that was transformed into the standardized score is ordinarily considered unusually small or unusually large and is labeled an outlier. This method of outlier detection ordinarily indicates more outliers than the box-plot method, although neither method indicates many.

II. PATTERNS THAT ARISE IN REPEATED SAMPLING

Samples and Statistics

It is often too difficult, too costly, or impossible to get complete information about an entire group we want to describe. For example, we are unable to determine the exact average age of all the secondary-school mathematics teachers in the United States because it is impossible for us to obtain all their ages. In such a case, we do the next best thing: we estimate the average using the ages of several dozen, several hundred, or several thousand carefully selected secondary-school mathematics teachers whom we believe are representative of the larger group. The entire group we want to learn about is called the *population,* and the subset of the population for which we have data is called the *sample* (and is represented by the letter *n*). In our example, the population would be the ages of all the secondary-school mathematics teachers in the United States and the sample would be the ages of those secondary-school mathematics teachers we are able to learn about.

As suggested in Section I, the mean of a population of measurements is the total of all the elements in the population divided by the number of elements used to get the total; the median is the middle value when the elements are ordered from low to high or high to low; and the standard deviation is the square root of the average of the squares of the distances that the elements are from the mean. We use the lowercase Greek letter mu, μ, to stand for a population's mean, the symbol M to stand for the median, and, as you have seen, the symbol σ to stand for the standard deviation. When μ M, and σ are unknown, as is frequently the case, we can use a sample n to estimate these quantities. For example, listed below in order from low to high are the ages of 50 $(=n)$ secondary-school mathematics teachers from throughout the United States who attended a statistics institute in Princeton, New Jersey. These 50 ages can be thought of as a sample from the population of ages of all the secondary-school mathematics teachers from across the United States.

26, 27, 29, 31, 31, 33, 34, 34, 35, 35,
36, 36, 36, 36, 37, 38, 39, 40, 40, 41,
41, 41, 42, 42, 43, 43, 43, 43, 44, 44,
44, 44, 45, 45, 46, 46, 47, 47, 47, 48,
48, 48, 49, 50, 51, 51, 52, 53, 54, 59.

The mean age, μ, and the median age, M, of the population of ages of all the secondary-school mathematics teachers from across the United States can be estimated by the mean of the ages in our sample (sample mean = $\bar{x}$), $\bar{x} = 41.88$ years, and by the median of the ages in our sample (sample median = m), $m = 43$ years. Letting $x_1, x_2, \ldots, x_n$ represent the data in our sample ($n = 50$), the sample mean ($\bar{x}$) may be written in *summation notation* as follows:

$$\bar{x} = \frac{1}{n} \sum_{i=1}^{n} x_i = \frac{(x_1 + x_2 + \cdots + x_n)}{n} = 41.88$$

For example,

$$\sum_{i=1}^{n} x_i = x_i + \cdots + x_n, \quad \sum_{i=2}^{4} x_i = x_2 + x_3 + x_4, \text{ and } \sum_{i=1}^{5}(x_i - \bar{x})^2 = (x_1 - \bar{x})^2 + (x_2 - \bar{x})^2 + \cdots + (x_5 - \bar{x})^2$$

(because complicated sums are encountered so frequently in this unit, we occasionally find it convenient to write them this way).

To estimate the population's standard deviation (σ), we apply the steps in Section I for computing σ, with two important modifications: *we use the data in the sample instead of the population and we divide by n–1 rather than* n. The first change is necessary because we are assuming that it is impossible to get all the data in the population. The reason for the second change is less obvious. Because the data in a sample, especially a small one, are not likely to include the extremes of the population—in our case, the youngest and oldest secondary-school teachers—it will have less variability than is actually present in the population. To adjust for this situation, we slightly inflate the *sample* standard deviation (s), thereby obtaining a better estimate of the *population's* standard deviation (σ). Thus, the formula we use to compute the sample standard deviation is as follows:

$$s = \sqrt{\frac{\sum\limits_{i=1}^{n}(x_i-\bar{x})^2}{n-1}} = \sqrt{\frac{(x_1-\bar{x})^2+(x_2-\bar{x})^2+\cdots+(x_n-\bar{x})^2}{n-1}}$$

Using this formula with the data above, our estimate of the population's standard deviation is $s = 7.26$ years. To compute the sample standard deviation using a calculator with statistical keys, use the key labeled s or $\sigma(n-1)$ or σ_{n-1} after entering all of the data.

To summarize, n refers to the size of the sample, and

μ = population mean	$\bar{x}$ = sample mean
M = population median	m = sample median
σ = pop. standard deviation	s = sample standard deviation

The numbers $\bar{x}$, m, and s are called *statistics*. A statistic is a function of the data in a sample. Other examples of statistics are the sample range (which is the largest number in a sample minus the smallest), the lower and upper quartiles of a sample (which are the medians of the ordered data less than and greater than the sample median), and the sample interquartile range (which is the upper quartile minus the lower quartile of a sample). The values of these statistics using the data in the math-teacher example are the following:

sample range = 59 – 26 = 33
sample lower quartile = 36
sample upper quartile = 47
sample interquartile range = 47 – 36 = 11

Now, let's see what might be revealed by creating a stem-and-leaf plot of the data. Either this plot or a line plot can give us a fairly accurate picture of what the population looks like if the sample is representative of the population.

Ages of 50 Secondary-School Teachers

2	679	Key: 2 ǀ 6 = 26 years
3	11344	
3	556666789	
4	001112233334444	
4	55667778889	
5	011234	
5	9	

The leaves on the plot form a graph that is roughly mound-shaped or bell-shaped—that is, the graph peaks in the middle (the early 40s) and gradually and symmetrically slopes down to the extremes (the 20s and the 50s). It is fairly common for a stem-and-leaf plot or a line plot of sample data to look like this. In these situations, the sample mean ($\bar{x}$) and the sample median (m) are likely to be very close to one another and, therefore, should be equally good estimates of the center of the population (which should be fairly symmetric itself); and the sample standard deviation (s) should be a good estimate of a "typical" deviation from the mean of the population. However, with any set of data (either a population or a sample), large measures of variability should make us look more carefully at how meaningful the measures of center might be. For the data in our example, the sample standard deviation (s) of approximately 7 years, along with the sample mean ($\bar{x}$) of approximately 42 years, suggests that it would not be unusual to see some ages up around 49 (approximately one sample standard deviation above the sample mean) and others down around 35 (one sample standard deviation below the sample mean). This idea will be discussed in much greater detail shortly.

Now, let's consider several other sets of data that represent samples from populations. We will explore the data by looking at stem-and-leaf plots, sample means, sample medians, and sample standard deviations. We want to practice and compare techniques for

a. Describing the shape of the data.

b. Describing the center of the data.

c. Describing the variability of the data.

Frequency of Absences

The list below is an account of the number of absences for each student in one section of a high school prealgebra class over a ten-week period.

$$5, 3, 8, 2, 42, 2, 8, 0, 11, 1, 0,$$
$$4, 39, 0, 0, 4, 7, 1, 42, 0, 1$$

The number of students (n) is 21. We will use the data from this class as a sample and explore what the absences in this particular section might tell us about the number of absences of all the students enrolled in that particular course in that school during the same ten-week period. Here is the stem-and-leaf plot of the data:

```
0 | 00000111        Key: 1 | 2 = 12 absences
0 | 223
0 | 445
0 | 7
0 | 88
1 | 1
1 |
1 |
1 |
1 |
2 |
2 |
2 |
2 |
2 |
3 |
3 |
3 |
3 |
3 | 9
4 |
4 | 22
```

Note: In this plot, we "spread" the stems to create more distance between the leaves. There are now five lines per stem—that is, each tens digit now has five lines instead of one. The 0 and 1 leaves go on the first line of each stem, the 2 and 3 leaves go on the second line, and so forth. We did this because most of the data cluster below 11.

Clearly, the stem-and-leaf plot is not mound-shaped. When a stem-and-leaf (or line) plot of data is not mound-shaped, the mean and median are unequal and the data are said to be *skewed*. If the mean exceeds the median, the data are said to be *skewed to the right*; and if the mean is less than the median, the data are said to be *skewed to the left*. When data are skewed to one end or the other, we sometimes describe their graph as being *J-shaped*. In the example above, the data are skewed to the right because the three unusually large numbers of absences inflate the sample mean in relation to the sample median. Calculating both of these numbers, we find the following:

$$\text{sample mean: } \bar{x} = 8.6$$
$$\text{sample median: } m = 3.0$$

Which is a better descriptor of the number of absences among the students in our sample? Because the sample mean and the sample median are very different—and only 4 of the 21 students were absent a number of times that exceeded the mean—it is clear that the sample median is a much better indicator of the approximate number of absences for most of the students in our sample. Thus, we would use the sample median, 3, to estimate the approximate number of absences for all of the students enrolled in prealgebra in that high school during that ten-week period.

The sample standard deviation (remember to divide by $n - 1$ instead of n) is $s = 13.9$. This number supposedly represents a "typical" number of days that the data differ from the sample mean. However, this number is quite large for data measuring absences over a ten-week period. Furthermore, it is not close to most typical deviations from the sample mean. Thus, it is not a good measure of variability in this case. The J-shaped distribution, the presence of unusual data (large in this case), and a standard deviation that is not close to typical deviations are all indicators that the sample median, rather than the sample mean, is the better measure of center for the sample data and that the sample median should be used to estimate the center of the population.

It is important to note that outliers in a sample are identified in essentially the same way in which they are identified in a population (see Section I): If a sample datum is two or more sample standard deviations below or above the sample mean, the datum is considered unusual and may be called an outlier—that is, a datum may be considered an outlier if it is less than (sample mean – 2(sample standard deviation)) or greater than (sample mean + 2(sample standard deviation)). Equivalently, a datum is an outlier if one of the following is true:

$$\frac{\text{datum} - \text{sample mean}}{\text{sample standard deviation}} \leq -2$$

$$\frac{\text{datum} - \text{sample mean}}{\text{sample standard deviation}} \geq 2$$

The box-plot method may also be used with sample data to identify outliers. By this method, any datum that falls outside the interval (sample LQ – 1.5(sample IQR), sample UQ + 1.5(sample IQR)) is called an outlier. Using the data in the previous example, we find that 39, 42, and 42 are outliers by both methods because in one case they exceed $\bar{x} + 2s = 8.6 + 2(13.9) = 36.4$ and in the other they exceed (sample UQ) + 1.5(sample IQR) = 8 + 1.5(7.5) = 19.25.

Prices of Dogs

Listed below is a sample of the asking prices of dogs for sale in the classified section of a newspaper.

Breed	Price
American Eskimo Husky	$150
American Eskimo Husky	175
Bassett Hound	150
Bassett Hound	250
Brittany Spaniel	300
Chesapeake	200
Cocker Spaniel	125
German Shepherd	225
Golden Retriever	295
Irish Setter	200
Lhasa Apso	75
Pekingese AKC	350
Pekingese non-AKC	150
Scottish Terrier	500
Siberian Husky	150
Terrier/Beagle mix	25
Yorkshire Terrier	150

Source: *Wisconsin State Journal*, April 30, 1989.

Let's draw a stem-and-leaf plot of the data.

Prices of Dogs in Classified Ads

```
0 | 2            Key: 1 | 2 = $120 to $129
0 | 7
1 | 2
1 | 555557
2 | 002
2 | 59
3 | 0
3 | 5
4 |
4 |
5 | 0
```

The graph is roughly mound-shaped, with the exception of one unusually high asking price that causes the sample mean, $\bar{x}$ = $204, to be quite a bit larger than the sample median, m = $175. The sample standard deviation is s = $112. The largest asking price, $500, is an outlier by either of the methods for detecting outliers, since it is greater than both $\bar{x} + 2s$ = $428 and (sample UQ) + 1.5(sample IQR) = $456.25. For this data, the sample standard deviation does represent the "typical" amount by which the data differ from the sample mean. While some of the data are fairly close to the sample mean, almost half (8 of 17) of the dogs for sale cost more than $50 less than the sample mean, with 2 costing much more than $100 less than the sample mean. On the other side of the data, we find that nearly a quarter of the dogs have asking prices from nearly $100 to $300 more than the sample mean. This much variability suggests that neither the sample mean nor the sample median may represent the data very well. The measures of center alone do not indicate that most of the dogs cost considerably more or considerably less than the sample mean and median, and it is important to be aware of this when analyzing data. Constructing a line plot or stem-and-leaf plot of the data makes it easier to recognize this variability, as does calculating various measures of variability.

Lodging Costs in Waikiki

The following list is a sample of the prices (in dollars) for one night's lodging in a standard double room in the Waikiki area of Honolulu.

53, 75, 45, 60, 89, 39, 60, 155, 95, 170, 65,
67, 85, 55, 32, 70, 80, 220, 320, 80, 85, 275,
75, 120, 86, 160, 80, 85, 90, 70, 90, 90

Source: *1991 Hawaii Accommodation Guide.*

1. Make a stem-and-leaf plot of the data.

2. Calculate the mean, median, and standard deviation of the sample data.

3. Discuss the shape of the graph and the presence of outliers.

4. How well do the sample mean and median describe the prices of hotel rooms included in the sample?

5. What does the sample standard deviation tell us about the sample mean and the data set as a whole?

6. Use the data in the sample to estimate the typical price for one night's lodging in a standard double room in Waikiki.

Comparing the Mean and Median of a Sample

Check your local newspaper to see if it gives birth weights, rainfall amounts, temperature extremes, or other similar data on a daily basis. If so, gather data for at least 20 days on one of these variables.

1. Make a stem-and-leaf plot of your data. If you use birth-weight data, it might be easier if you convert the data (conventionally given in pounds and ounces) to ounces or round it to the nearest tenth of a pound. Is your plot mound-shaped? Do you suspect that the sample mean and median will be fairly close together?

2. Calculate the mean, median, and standard deviation of your sample data.

3. Does your sample contain any outliers?

4. Are the sample mean and median good measures of the center of the data?

5. What does the sample standard deviation tell about the sample mean and the data as a whole?

Random Samples

The ages of the 50 secondary-school mathematics teachers (in the first example of this section) may not fairly represent the ages of all secondary-school mathematics teachers across the United States. Perhaps older teachers (those nearing retirement) were not selected for the institute. The absence of older ages would bias the sample toward the younger ages. Similarly, the sample of asking prices for dogs may not fairly represent the asking prices of all dogs for sale in Madison, Wisconsin, at this time. (Why?) How do we, then, get samples that fairly represent the population we want to study? One way is to choose *random* samples.

Suppose a teacher wants to select a random sample of five students from a class. One way to do this would be to put each name on a slip of paper, mix the slips up in a box, and draw out five. Another way (which is much more convenient for large populations) would be to use a random number table like the one shown on the following page. A random number table displays the digits 0 through 9 in random order. To select a random sample of 5 students from a class of 25, first assign each student a number from 1 to 25. Pick an arbitrary starting place on the random number table and begin to read off pairs of digits from these, going either left, right, up, or down from your starting point. (It doesn't matter which way you go, as long as you decide on a direction before you look at the table.) Disregard any pair of digits that is greater than 25. Continue until you have found 5 numbers between 01 and 25—these are your 5 randomly selected students.

Application 17 provides some experience in selecting random samples and observing how they compare to nonrandom samples. Random samples produced by manipulatives (dice and spinners) are considered thereafter.

Table of Random Numbers									
39634	62349	74088	65564	16379	19713	39153	69459	17986	24537
14595	35050	40469	27478	44526	67331	93365	54526	22356	93208
30734	71571	83722	79712	25775	65178	07763	82928	31131	30196
64628	89126	91254	24090	25752	03091	39411	73146	06089	15630
42831	95113	43511	42082	15140	34733	68076	18292	69486	80468
80583	70361	41047	26792	78466	03395	17635	09697	82447	31405
00209	90404	99457	72570	42194	49043	24330	14939	09865	45906
05409	20830	01911	60767	55248	79253	12317	84120	77772	50103
95836	22530	91785	80210	34361	52228	33869	94332	83868	61672
65358	70469	87149	89509	72176	18103	55169	79954	72002	20582
72249	04037	36192	40221	14918	53437	60571	40995	55006	10694
41692	40581	93050	48734	34652	41577	04631	49184	39295	81776
61885	50796	96822	82002	07973	52925	75467	86013	98072	91942
48917	48129	48624	48248	91465	54898	61220	18721	67387	66575
88378	84299	12193	03785	49314	39761	99132	28775	45276	91816
77800	25734	09801	92087	02955	12872	89848	48579	06028	13827
24028	03405	01178	06316	81916	40170	53665	87202	88628	47121
86558	84750	43994	01760	96205	27937	45416	71964	52261	30781
78545	49201	05329	14182	10971	90472	44682	39304	19819	55799
14969	64623	82780	35686	30941	14622	04126	25498	95452	63937
58697	31973	06303	94202	62287	56164	79157	98375	24558	99241
38449	46438	91579	01907	72146	05764	22400	94490	49833	09258
62134	87244	73348	80114	78490	64735	31010	66975	28652	36166
72749	13347	65030	26128	49067	27904	49953	74674	94617	13317
81638	36566	42709	33717	59943	12027	46547	61303	46699	76243
46574	79670	10342	89543	75030	23428	29541	32501	89422	87474
11873	57196	32209	67663	07990	12288	59245	83638	23642	61715
13862	72778	09949	23096	01791	19472	14634	31690	36602	62943
08312	27886	82321	28666	72998	22514	51054	22940	31842	54245
11071	44430	94664	91294	35163	05494	32882	23904	41340	61185
82509	11842	86963	50307	07510	32545	90717	46856	86079	13769
07426	67341	80314	58910	93948	85738	69444	09370	58194	28207
57696	25592	91221	95386	15857	84645	89659	80535	93233	82798
08074	89810	48521	90740	02687	83117	74920	25954	99629	78978
20128	53721	01518	40699	20849	04710	38989	91322	56057	58573

Understanding the Role of Randomization in Collecting Data

Why do we emphasize *random* samples when we are concerned about how well sample results reflect the nature of the population being studied? The answer is that random samples produce results that conform to fairly predictable patterns and yield estimates that tend to be *unbiased* (centering at the numbers being estimated). On the other hand, samples taken by personal judgment usually have no predictable patterns and tend to yield estimates that are *biased* (centering to one side of the numbers being estimated). The following activity compares the behavior of random samples with the behavior of judgmental samples.

Instructions

1. Keep the sheet of rectangles at the end of this application covered until your teacher gives the signal to begin. Then, look at the sheet for ten seconds (your teacher will keep the time) and write down your guess as to the average area of the rectangles on the page. (The unit of measure is the underlying square on the graph paper. Thus, rectangle 33 has area $4 \times 3 = 12$.)

2. Select five different rectangles that, in your judgment, are representative of the rectangles on the page. Write down their numbers and their areas. Compute the average area of the five and compare it to your guess.

3. Now, select five more rectangles (all different from the first five) that, in your judgment, represent the rectangles on the page. Write down their numbers and their areas. Compute the average area of the second set of five areas and compare it to your guess.

4. Compute the average of the areas of the ten rectangles in your two judgmental samples combined. Compare it to your guess. Which estimate of the average area do you like best —your guess, the two averages of five rectangle, or the average of ten rectangles? Why?

Analysis

1. As a class, collect the guesses, the first average of five rectangles, the second average of five rectangles, and the average of ten rectangles from each student. Working together, plot each of the four data sets on a line plot and discuss any patterns or trends that you see in the results.

2. Using a random-number table and working on your own, select a random sample of five different rectangles from the sheet. (Pick an arbitrary starting place on the random number table and begin reading off groups of three digits until you find 5 that are between 001 and 100.) Record the areas of the corresponding rectangles, and compute the average area. (If a rectangle already selected is chosen a second time, discard it and use a new random number to select a different rectangle.)

3. Use the procedure in the previous problem to select a second random sample of five different rectangles, with no repetitions from the first sample, and compute the average area.

4. Combine the two random samples, each of size five, into one random sample of ten rectangles. Compute the average area of the ten sampled rectangles.

5. As with the judgmental samples, collect the data as a class and construct line plots of the two sets of averages of five rectangles and the set of averages of ten rectangles.

6. Compare the line plots from the guesses, the judgmental samples, and the random samples. Discuss any differences or similarities that you see in these plots.

Discussion

1. Your teacher has the true average (mean) value for the areas of the rectangles on the page. After obtaining this value, discuss and compare the notion of bias in judgmental samples and random samples.

2. If someone told you that he or she did not need to randomly select the respondents to a survey because personal judgment was just as good (or perhaps even better), what would you say?

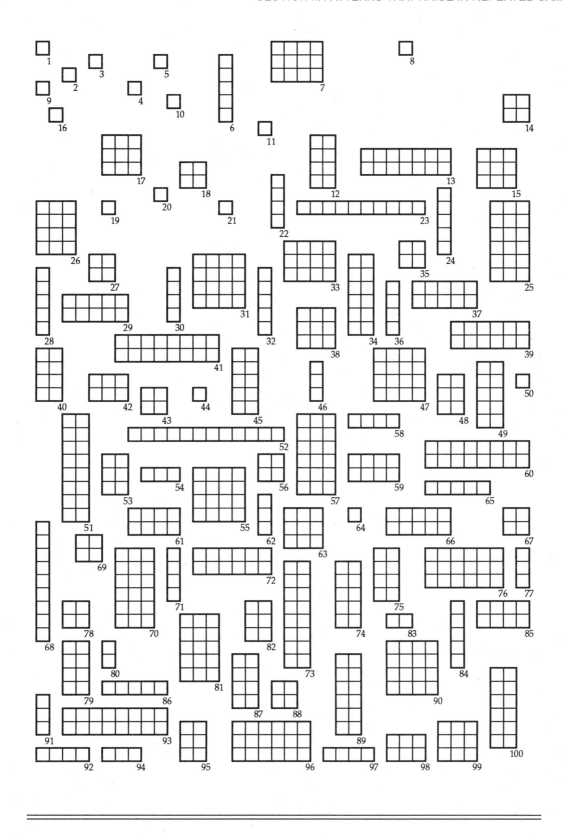

Means of Random Samples

In the game of Aggravation®, two to six players consecutively move each of their four marbles around a game board, from base to home. The first player to get all four marbles home is declared the winner. The number of slots that a player may move a marble across, in turn, is determined by the roll of one standard (fair) six-faced die (die is the singular of dice). What makes this game so aggravating is that if player A's marble lands on a slot occupied by player B's marble, player B must return his or her marble to base. To restart his or her marble, player B must roll either a 1 or a 6. Once a marble is started, moving it home quickly is to a player's advantage. To do this, a player would have to consistently roll lots of 4s, 5s, and 6s. How unusual is it to average 4 or more per roll over 20 or 30 rolls, or more? By exploring the behavior of sample means through some simple experiments with dice, random digits, and spinners, you will learn how to answer this and other similar questions.

Suppose that you roll a fair die one time. The outcome of the roll—which might be a 3, for example—can be thought of as a *random sample of size 1* from the population represented by all possible rolls of the die. We will never see this population because to do so we would have to roll the die an infinite number of times. However, our knowledge of probability suggests what the population should look like. Since the die is fair, in the long run roughly $\frac{1}{6}$ of the rolls should be 1s, $\frac{1}{6}$ should be 2s, and so on. If you take 5 more samples of size 1—that is, roll the die 5 more times—will your set of 6 numbers contain each of the numbers 1, 2, 3, 4, 5, and 6? Probably not, although it might! If it did, you would have observed an *ideal sample*. An ideal sample is a sample that produces exactly the same outcomes in exactly the same proportions as the population. An ideal sample perfectly reflects the population: the mean, median, and variability in an ideal sample are the same as the mean, median, and variability in the population. Thus, an ideal sample of size 12 from the population represented by a fair die will contain two 1s, two 2s, . . . , and two 6s. The mean and median of this sample, both 3.5, equal the mean and median of the population. The standard deviation of the population, $\sigma = \sqrt{\frac{35}{12}}$, is computed from the ideal sample using the following formula:

$$\sigma = \sqrt{\frac{(x_1 - \mu)^2 + (x_2 - \mu)^2 + \cdots + (x_n - \mu)^2}{n}},$$

In this formula, $n = 12$; $x_1, \ldots, x_n$ are the elements in the ideal sample; and the population mean (μ) is the mean of the ideal sample. It is impossible to have an ideal sample of size ten from the population represented by a fair die because each of the six elements of the population cannot appear the same number of times.

This Sample Is Ideal!

1. List the elements in an ideal sample of size 6 from the population represented by a fair die. Use this data to find the mean, median, and standard deviation of the population.

2. List the elements in an ideal sample of size 18 from the population represented by a fair die. Use this data to find the mean, median, and standard deviation of the population.

3. Compare the values of the population mean, median, and standard deviation that you found in problems 1 and 2 with those values computed from an ideal sample of size 12 and given in the discussion preceding this application. Describe the pattern(s) that you observe.

4. An ideal sample of size 600 is taken from the population represented by a fair die. What are the mean, median, and standard deviation of the population?

5. Let us suppose that the number of elements in an ideal sample from the population represented by a fair die is some multiple of 6. What are the values of the population mean, median, and standard deviation? Can you prove your conjecture? (This problem is more difficult.)

A table of random numbers consists of the digits 0, 1, 2, ... , 9, arranged so that in the long run if you move randomly from one digit to another each digit will occur about the same number of times. Such a table is provided on page 60 An individual digit selected from a random location on this table can be considered a sample of size 1 from the population represented by the table of random numbers.

6. List the elements in an ideal sample of size 10 from the population represented by the table of random numbers. Use this data to find the mean, median, and standard deviation of the population.

7. Repeat problem 6 using an ideal sample of size 20.

8. Repeat problem 6 using an ideal sample of size 30.

9. Compare your answers to problems 6–8. Describe the pattern that you see. Without doing any computations, what are the mean, median, and standard deviation of the population represented by the table of random numbers if an ideal sample of size 600 is used to compute these quantities?

10. Without doing any computations, what are the mean, median, and standard deviation of the population if an ideal sample size is any multiple of 10?

11. Is it possible to have an ideal sample of size 23 from this population? Why?

You can use the spinner on the following page by spinning a paper clip around the point of a pencil. If you repeatedly spin the spinner and record the number of the region where the spinner stops each time, in the long run you should observe about twice as

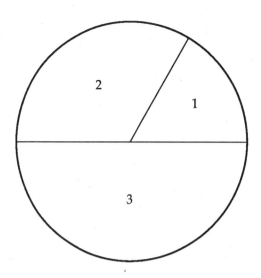

many 2s as 1s and three times as many 3s as 1s. A digit recorded after a single spin can be considered a sample of size 1 from the population represented by the spinner.

12. List the elements in the smallest possible ideal sample from the population represented by the spinner and use this data to find the mean, median, and standard deviation of the population.

13. List the elements in an ideal sample of size 18 from the population represented by the spinner and use this data to find the mean, median, and standard deviation of the population. How do these 3 numbers compare with the 3 that you found in problem 12?

14. Give a general statement describing the number of data elements that must be in an ideal sample from the population represented by the spinner. What are the values of the population mean, median, and standard deviation for any ideal sample? Can you prove your conjecture?

15. Is it possible to have an ideal sample of size 15 from this population? Why?

Sample Means in Repeated Sampling

By exploring line plots of means computed from samples that are repeatedly selected from a population, we can get a glimpse of how the distribution of sample means changes as the sample size increases. Let's begin by comparing the line plots of sample means for 20 samples of size 1 ($n = 1$), 20 samples of size 2 ($n = 2$), and 20 samples of size 3 ($n = 3$) from the population represented by a fair die. When $n = 1$, the data themselves are means. A single sample mean is obtained by rolling one die once. By repeating this 20 times, 20 means based on samples of size 1 are generated:

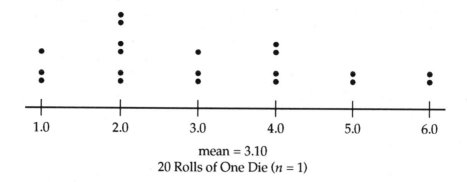

mean = 3.10
20 Rolls of One Die ($n = 1$)

We see that these means are centered fairly close to 3.5, the population mean, and that they are spread out across all the possible values that we might see when rolling a fair die one time. Suppose you were to take another 20 samples of size 1 from this population. Would a line plot of your data look exactly like the previous one and would the average (mean) of your data equal 3.10, the average (mean) of the first 20 means? The answer to both of these questions is probably no. However, your line plot, like ours, will probably have roughly equal numbers of 1s, 2s, . . . , and 6s; and, consequently, the average (mean) of your data is not likely to differ much from 3.5.

When $n = 2$, a single sample mean is obtained by rolling two dice once or a single die twice and then computing the mean of the two numbers. Repeat this process 20 times to generate 20 means based on samples of size 2.

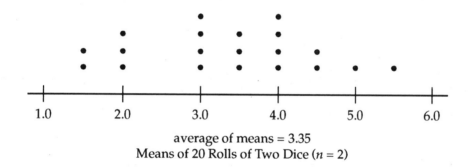

average of means = 3.35
Means of 20 Rolls of Two Dice ($n = 2$)

When $n = 2$, the sample means are still centered near 3.5; but they are less spread out and more mound-shaped than the sample means when $n = 1$. In fact, the most extreme values that a mean can have—namely, 1 and 6—are not even present, suggesting that these values are more unlikely in averages of size 2 than in averages of size 1.

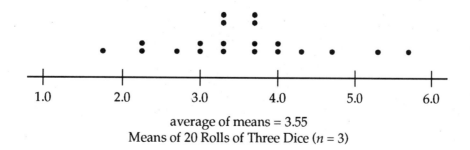

average of means = 3.55
Means of 20 Rolls of Three Dice ($n = 3$)

When $n = 3$, the sample means are again still centered at 3.5. They are even less vari-able and more mound-shaped than the sample means when $n = 1$ and $n = 2$, and the average (mean) of our 20 means is 3.55. A pattern seems to be emerging!

Because it is a rather tedious process to take samples, compute the sample means, and then draw line plots, we have thus far confined our investigation to small sets of means based on samples of size $n = 1, 2,$ and 3. Besides being time-consuming, this approach has another disadvantage: with only a small number of sample means comput-ed using small sample sizes, it is difficult to get a broad picture of how sample means distribute themselves around the population mean in repeated sampling. To get a better picture of what happens, we used a computer to generate sets of 100 sample means based on samples of size $n = 1, 2, 3, 4, 5, 10, 20,$ and 30. Line plots for these data are dis-played on the following pages. The average (mean) of each set of means is given with each plot. As you compare these figures, you can see what happens as the sample size that is used to compute the means increases: the distribution of the sample means tends to be less variable and more symmetrically clustered around the population mean, and the average for each set of means tends to get closer to the population mean.

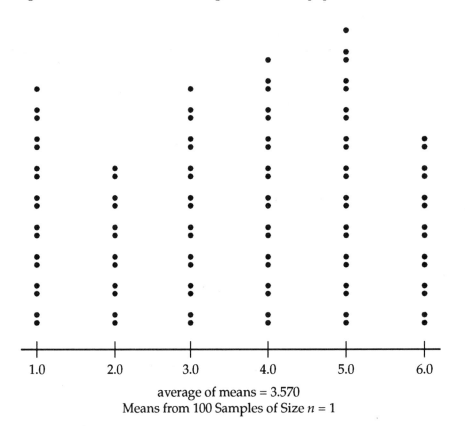

average of means = 3.570
Means from 100 Samples of Size $n = 1$

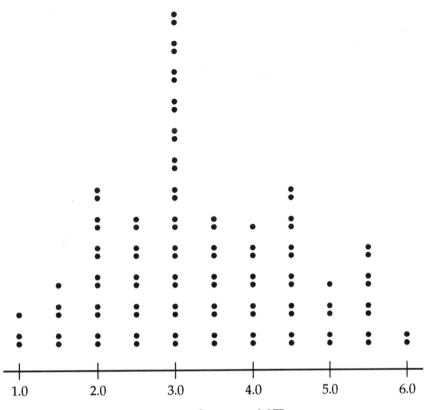

average of means = 3.375
Means from 100 Samples of Size $n = 2$

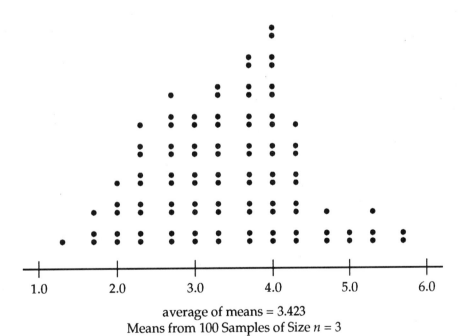

average of means = 3.423
Means from 100 Samples of Size $n = 3$

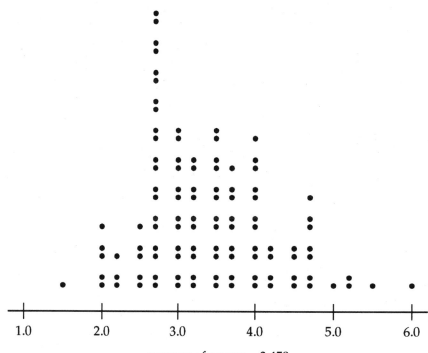

average of means = 3.458
Means from 100 Samples of Size $n = 4$

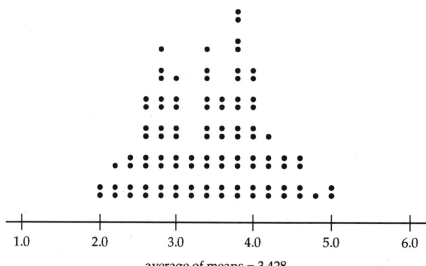

average of means = 3.428
Means from 100 Samples of Size $n = 5$

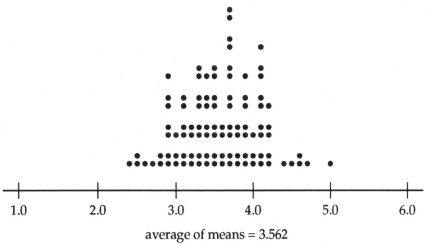

average of means = 3.562
Means from 100 Samples of Size $n = 10$

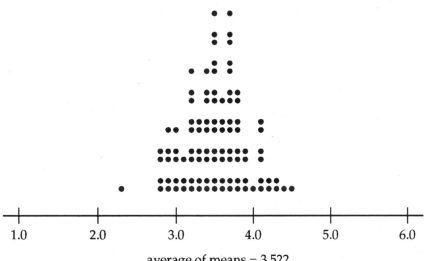

average of means = 3.522
Means from 100 Samples of Size $n = 20$

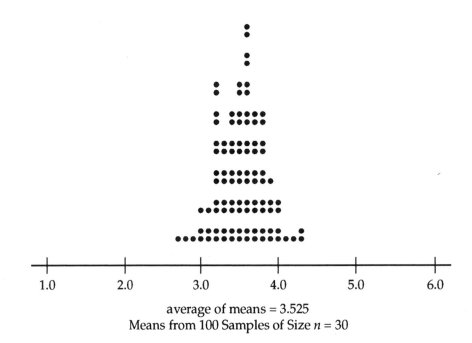

average of means = 3.525
Means from 100 Samples of Size $n = 30$

You may recall that the reason we started this investigation of sample means was to try to answer a question about the game Aggravation®, namely, how unusual is it to average 4 or more per roll of a fair die over 20 or 30 rolls, or more? We can now give a partial answer to that question.

Look again at the line plot showing 100 sample means obtained for samples of size $n = 20$. For this data, only 13 out of 100 means are 4 or larger (count the dots!). Thus, we would estimate the probability of averaging at least 4 per roll over 20 rolls of a fair die to be only 0.13. Similarly, counting the dots on the line plot for samples of size $n = 30$, you will find only 8 of the 100 means are 4 or larger. So, the estimated probability of averaging at least 4 per roll over 30 rolls of a fair die is only 0.08. (This is *another* reason for calling the game Aggravation®!) A second answer to the Aggravation® player's question is given later in this section.

Now, let's explore the behavior of sample means when populations with different distributional shapes are repeatedly sampled. Will distributions of sample means still tend to be less variable and more symmetrically clustered around the population mean? Will the mean of a set of means still get closer to the population mean as the size of the samples gets large? The next three applications should help you answer these questions.

The Behavior of Sample Means When Sampling the Population of Random Digits

Use the table of random numbers on page 60 to do the problems in this application. Refer to Application 18 for details on how to sample this population.

1. Generate 10 samples of size $n = 1$ and make a line plot of these data. Compare your plot and the mean of your data to a line plot and the mean of an ideal sample. If you generated another 10 samples of size n = 1, would a line plot of your new data look exactly like the line plot of your first set of data and would the mean of your second set of data equal the mean of your first set of data? Why?

For the next two questions, combine your data with data obtained by other students.

2. Generate 10 samples of size $n = 2$ and compute the mean of each sample. Draw a line plot and compute the mean of your 10 sample means. Compare your line plot and the mean of your data to a line plot and the mean of an ideal sample. Describe what you see. Are averages as small as 0 or as large as 9 as likely for samples of size $n = 2$ as for samples of size $n = 1$? Why? Estimate the probability that the mean of 2 randomly selected digits will exceed 6.

3. Generate 10 samples of size $n = 3$ and compute the mean of each sample. Draw a line plot and compute the mean of your 10 sample means. Compare this line plot with the line plots of sample means when $n = 1$ and $n = 2$ (see problems 1 and 2). Describe what you see. Is a pattern emerging? If so, what is it? Estimate the probability that the mean of 3 randomly selected digits will exceed 6.

4. Using a computer, we selected 100 samples, each of size $n = 10$, from the population of random numbers. A line plot of the sample means appears below. How does the shape of this plot differ from the shapes of your plots in each of the three previous problems? Estimate the probability that the mean of 10 randomly selected digits will exceed 6. Compare this estimate to your estimates in problems 2 and 3. Explain why your estimates are different.

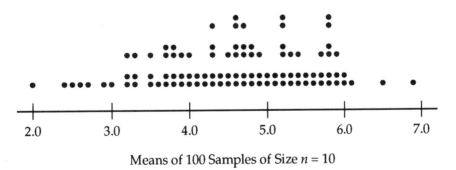

Means of 100 Samples of Size $n = 10$

The Behavior of Sample Means When a Population's Elements Are Unequally Likely—Part 1

All the examples you have investigated so far have involved fair dice and random digits, both of which generate equally likely outcomes. In this application, you will generate data from the population represented by the spinner described in Application 18. With this approach, you can begin to see first-hand that the behavior of sample means in repeated sampling does *not* depend on equally likely outcomes.

1. Get 10 samples of size $n = 1$ and make a line plot of your data. Compare your plot and the mean of your data to a line plot and the mean of an ideal sample.

To answer the questions in the next problem, you may wish to generate additional data yourself or to combine your data with data obtained by other students.

2. Generate 10 samples of size $n = 2$ and compute the mean of each sample. Draw a line plot of your 10 sample means and compute their average (mean). Compare your line plot and mean to the line plot and mean of an ideal sample. Describe what you see. Are averages as small as 1 or as large as 3 as likely for samples of size $n = 2$ as for samples of size $n = 1$? Why? Estimate the probability that the mean of a sample of size 2 will be at least 2.5.

3. Ten samples of size $n = 3$ from this spinner, with the calculated sample means, are given in the following table. How does the line plot of the means shown below compare with your line plots for problems 1 and 2? How does the average of the sample means compare with the population mean? Estimate the probability that the mean of a sample of size $n = 3$ will be at least 2.5.

Spin	First Value	Second Value	Third Value	Mean
1	2	2	3	7/3 = 2.33
2	2	3	2	7/3 = 2.33
3	2	3	1	2 = 2.00
4	3	3	3	3 = 3.00
5	3	3	3	3 = 3.00
6	3	3	1	7/3 = 2.33
7	1	2	1	4/3 = 1.33
8	2	3	2	7/3 = 2.33
9	3	3	2	8/3 = 2.67
10	3	3	3	3 = 3.00

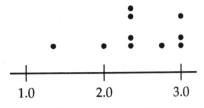

Means of Ten Samples of Size *n* = 3

4. Using a computer, 100 samples of size *n* = 10 were selected from the population. The 100 sample means are plotted below. Describe the shape of the distribution.

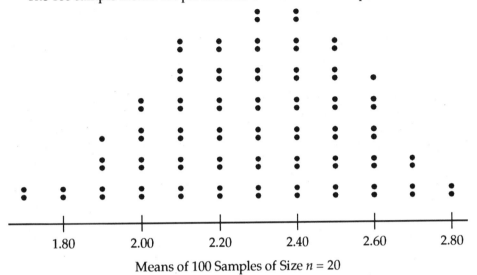

Means of 100 Samples of Size *n* = 20

Means from 100 samples of size n = 20 are shown below. Compare this plot to the one above for samples of size 10.

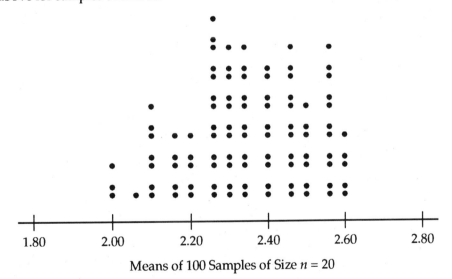

Means of 100 Samples of Size *n* = 20

Means from 100 samples of size *n* = 30 are shown following. Compare this plot to the ones above for samples of size *n* = 10 and *n* = 20.

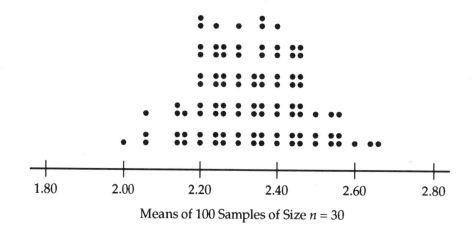

Means of 100 Samples of Size $n = 30$

5. Use the line plots in problem 4 to estimate the probability that the mean of a sample of size n from the population represented by the spinner will be at least 2.5 when $n = 10, 20,$ and 30. Describe and explain the pattern you see.

Application 21

The Behavior of Sample Means When a Population's Elements Are Unequally Likely—Part 2

If you repeatedly spin the following spinner and record the number in the region where the spinner stops each time, in the long run you should observe about the same number of 1s, 2s, and 15s; and the number of 0s should be about the same as the total number of 1s, 2s, and 15s. A value recorded after a single spin can be considered a sample of size 1 from the population represented by the spinner.

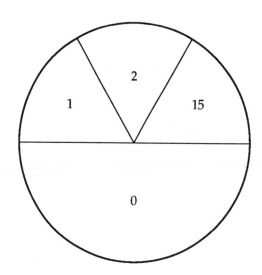

1. What is the fewest number of elements that can be in an ideal sample from the population represented by this spinner? List them and then use these data to find the mean and median of the population.

2. Draw a line plot of the ideal sample and describe the shape of the population.

3. Which measure of center—the mean or the median—most accurately indicates the middle of the population?

To answer the questions in the next problem, you may wish to generate additional data yourself or to combine your data with those generated by other students.

4. Generate 10 samples of size $n = 2$ and compute the mean of each sample. Draw a line plot of your 10 sample means. Are averages as small as 0 or as large as 15 as likely for samples of size $n = 2$ as for samples of size $n = 1$? Why?

5. Line plots of means computed from 100 samples of size $n = 10$ and 100 samples of size $n = 20$ follow. Describe how the shape of the sampling distribution of means changes as the sample size increases. Explain why there is still so much variability among the means computed from samples of size $n = 10$.

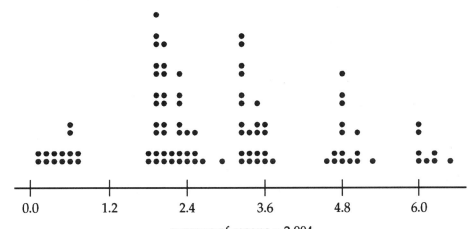

average of means = 2.994
Means of 100 Samples of Size $n = 10$

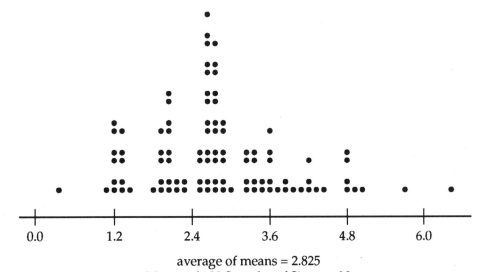

average of means = 2.825
Means of 100 Samples of Size $n = 20$

(Gaps in these plots exist because the population is extremely skewed.)

Discussion Questions

1. The mean of an ideal sample from a certain population is μ. Samples of size n are repeatedly selected from the population and the mean of each sample is computed and located on a line plot. How is the shape of the line plot influenced by the sample size, n? Does your answer depend on whether a line plot of an ideal sample is symmetric? Explain.

2. Is the mean of a single sample of size $n = 10$ more or less likely to be close to the population mean than if $n = 20$? Why? Does your answer depend on whether a line plot of an ideal sample is symmetric? Explain.

A Practical Rule on the Behavior of Sample Means

You have learned that as the size of the sample, n, is increased in repeated sampling, sets of sample means tend to become more mound-shaped, less variable, and more centered around the population mean regardless of the shape of the population. Do these changes occur in a predictable fashion? Is it possible to estimate the proportion of means falling within one or more sample standard deviations of the mean of all of the means? Is there a relationship between the variability in a set of means, the variability in the population, and the size of the samples? Let's explore a few examples involving sampling from the population represented by a fair die to see if you can find answers to some of these questions.

Below and on the next page are 7 of the sets of 100 sample means each that were used to form the line plots on pages 69–72. Frequency counts of the means based on samples of size $n = 2, 3, 4, 5,$ and 10 are followed by stem-and-leaf plots for the means based on samples of size $n = 20$ and $n = 30$. At the end is a table giving the sample mean and standard deviation for each set of means. The symbols $\bar{\bar{x}}$ and $s_{\bar{x}}$ are used to emphasize that the sample mean and standard deviation are computed from a set of sample means.

$n = 2$		$n = 3$		$n = 4$		$n = 5$		$n = 10$	
Average of Means	Frequency of Occurence	Average of Means	Frequency of Occurence	Average of Means	Frequency of Occurence	Average of Means	Frequency of Occurence	Average of Means	Frequency of Occurence
1.0	3	1.33	1	1.50	1	2.0	2	2.4	1
1.5	5	1.67	3	1.75	0	2.2	3	2.5	2
2.0	12	2.00	5	2.00	5	2.4	4	2.6	1
2.5	10	2.33	9	2.25	3	2.4	8	2.7	1
3.0	24	2.67	11	2.50	5	2.8	11	2.8	2
3.5	10	3.00	10	2.75	16	3.0	9	2.9	7
4.0	9	3.33	12	3.00	10	3.2	4	3.0	3
4.5	12	3.67	14	3.25	8	3.4	11	3.1	6
5.0	5	4.00	16	3.50	12	3.6	8	3.2	4
5.5	8	4.33	9	3.75	9	3.8	14	3.3	8
6.0	2	4.67	3	4.00	11	4.0	10	3.4	7
		5.00	2	4.25	4	4.2	5	3.5	8
		5.33	3	4.50	4	4.4	4	3.6	4
		5.67	2	4.75	7	4.6	4	3.7	12
				5.00	1	4.8	1	3.8	4
				5.25	2	5.0	2	3.9	7
				5.50	1			4.0	3
				5.75	0			4.1	9
				6.00	1			4.2	5
								4.3	0
								4.4	1
								4.5	1
								4.6	2
								4.7	1
								5.0	1

Frequency Counts of Means Based on Samples of Size $n = 2, 3, 4, 5,$ and 10

$n = 20$	
2.3	5
2.4	
2.5	
2.6	
2.7	
2.8	0005
2.9	00555
3.0	00055
3.1	0005
3.2	00005555
3.3	055555
3.4	000555555
3.5	0000000555555
3.6	000000055555
3.7	00055555
3.8	00000555
3.9	0555
4.0	0555
4.1	00055
4.2	
4.3	00
4.4	0
4.5	0

2.3 | 5 = 2.35

$n = 30$	
2.7	3
2.8	0
2.9	06
3.0	33
3.1	0036666
3.2	033333336666
3.3	003366666
3.4	00333666
3.5	0033333336666666666
3.6	00033366
3.7	000033336666
3.8	000033666
3.9	336
4.0	003
4.1	3
4.2	0
4.3	33

2.7 | 3 = 2.73
2.9 | 6 = 2.96

Stem-And-Leaf Plots of Means Based on Samples of Size $n = 20$ and $n = 30$

	$n = 2$	$n = 3$	$n = 4$	$n = 5$	$n = 10$	$n = 20$	$n = 30$
Ave. of Means ($\bar{\bar{x}}$)	3.375	3.423	3.458	3.428	3.562	3.522	3.525
Sample Std. Dev. of the Means ($s_{\bar{x}}$)	1.232	0.937	0.876	0.704	0.518	0.399	0.312

Sample Mean and Standard Deviation for Each Set of Means

Consider the set of 100 sample means based on samples of size $n = 2$. How many of the means fall within one or two sample standard deviations of their mean? Because $\bar{\bar{x}} = 3.375$ and $s_{\bar{x}} = 1.232$, these questions are equivalent to asking; How many means are in $(\bar{\bar{x}} - s_{\bar{x}}, \bar{\bar{x}} + s_{\bar{x}}) = (2.143, 4.607)$ and how many are in $(\bar{\bar{x}} - 2s_{\bar{x}}, \bar{\bar{x}} + 2s_{\bar{x}}) = (0.911, 5.839)$? By counting, you will find the answers to be 65 and 98, respectively. The following table gives these intervals and the number of sample means they contain for each of the 7 sets of 100 sample means given above. Do you see a pattern?

n	I_1	Number of Means in I_1	I_2	Number of Means in I_2
2	(2.143, 4.607)	65	(0.911, 5.839)	98
3	(2.486, 4.360)	72	(1.549, 5.297)	94
4	(2.582, 4.334)	70	(1.706, 5.210)	95
5	(2.724, 4.132)	67	(2.020, 4.836)	96
10	(3.044, 4.080)	63	(2.526, 4.598)	93
20	(3.123, 3.921)	66	(2.724, 4.320)	97
30	(3.213, 3.837)	73	(2.901, 4.149)	94

$$I_1 = (\bar{\bar{x}} - s_{\bar{x}}, \bar{\bar{x}} + s_{\bar{x}}) \quad I_2 = (\bar{\bar{x}} - 2s_{\bar{x}}, \bar{\bar{x}} + 2s_{\bar{x}})$$

Number of Means within One and Two Sample Standard Deviations of the Sample Mean

The data in the preceding table indicate that sets of sample means obtained by repeatedly sampling the population, represented by a fair, die cluster around their average (mean) in a fairly predictable manner: about 68% of the means in each set of means are within one sample standard deviation of the average of all the means in the set and about 95% of them are within two sample standard deviations. Indeed, for our data, the average of the numbers of means falling within one sample standard deviation of the average of all the means for all seven sets of data (that is, $(65 + 72 + \ldots + 73)/7)$) is 68 and the average number of means falling within two sample standard deviations is 95.3. Furthermore, 100% of the means in each set are within three sample standard deviations of their average. This consistent pattern of clustering is not unique to the seven sets of means that we happened to generate on a computer. *Provided that the line plot of the data is approximately mound-shaped* (as it is when you are working with sets of sample means), the following will always be the case:

1. About 68% of the data will fall within one sample standard deviation of the sample mean.

2. About 95% of the data will fall within two sample standard deviations of the sample mean.

3. Essentially all the data will be within three sample standard deviations of the sample mean.

These observations are so important in basic statistics that they are collectively called *the empirical rule.*

The generality of the empirical rule needs to be emphasized. Notice that it applies to *any* set of data *provided that the line plot of the data is roughly mound-shaped.* Suppose you had a sample of n numbers from some population. If you view each number as a mean of a sample of size 1 from the population, then the sample mean and standard deviation, $\bar{x}$ and s, correspond to the sample mean and standard deviation of a set of means. Consequently, for your sample of n numbers, intervals of the form $(\bar{x} - s, \bar{x} + s)$, $(\bar{x} - 2s, \bar{x} + 2s)$, and $(\bar{x} - 3s, \bar{x} + 3s)$ should respectively contain about 68%, 95%, and essentially all of the data in your sample, *provided a line plot of the data is roughly mound-shaped.* For example, consider the batting averages of the American League batting champions from 1941–91 that were displayed on p. 45–46. A line plot and a box plot for these data appear below. Although the data appear to be fairly mound-shaped, it is clear that they are slightly skewed to the right. For these data, 37 out of 51 batting averages ($\approx 73\%$) fall in the interval $(\bar{x} - s, \bar{x} + s) = (.322, .365)$, 47 out of 51 batting averages ($\approx 92\%$) fall in the interval $(\bar{x} - 2s, \bar{x} + 2s) = (.300, .387)$, and all of the data fall in $(\bar{x} - 3s, \bar{x} + 3s) = (.278, .408)$. Observe that the empirical rule fairly accurately describes how the data are spread out around the mean even though the data are slightly skewed!

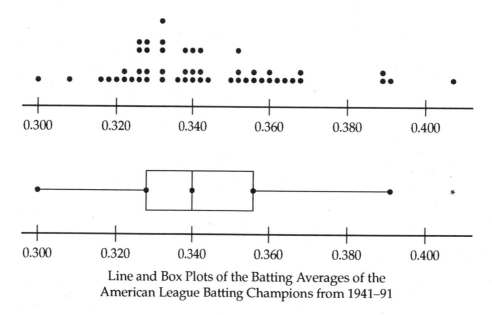

Line and Box Plots of the Batting Averages of the
American League Batting Champions from 1941–91

Application 22

The Empirical Rule

1. A set of data consists of the means of 50 samples of size $n = 2$ from the population of random digits. If $\bar{\bar{x}}$ is the average and $s_{\bar{x}}$ is the standard deviation of this set of sample means, approximately how many of the sample means will be in $(\bar{\bar{x}} - s_{\bar{x}}, \bar{\bar{x}} + s_{\bar{x}})$? In $(\bar{\bar{x}} - 2s_{\bar{x}}, \bar{\bar{x}} + 2s_{\bar{x}})$? In $(\bar{\bar{x}} - 3s_{\bar{x}}, \bar{\bar{x}} + 3s_{\bar{x}})$? Does the empirical rule apply to this data? Why? Would the empirical rule work better if the size of the samples was larger?

2. A set of data consists of the means of 200 samples of size $n = 2$ from the population represented by the spinner in Application 18 (p. 66). Using the empirical rule, approximately how many of your sample means will be in each of the intervals: $(\bar{\bar{x}} - s_{\bar{x}}, \bar{\bar{x}} + s_{\bar{x}})$, $(\bar{\bar{x}} - 2s_{\bar{x}}, \bar{\bar{x}} + 2s_{\bar{x}})$, and $(\bar{\bar{x}} - 3s_{\bar{x}}, \bar{\bar{x}} + 3s_{\bar{x}})$? Does the empirical rule apply to these data? Why?

3. Below is a stem-and-leaf plot of the means of 100 samples of size $n = 2$ from the population represented by the spinner in Application 18. The sample mean and standard deviation for this set of data are 2.365 and 0.5118, respectively. Does the empirical rule apply to these data? Find the endpoints of the intervals $(\bar{\bar{x}} - s_{\bar{x}}, \bar{\bar{x}} + s_{\bar{x}})$, $(\bar{\bar{x}} - 2s_{\bar{x}}, \bar{\bar{x}} + 2s_{\bar{x}})$, and $(\bar{\bar{x}} - 3s_{\bar{x}}, \bar{\bar{x}} + 3s_{\bar{x}})$ and count the number of means falling in each. Compare your results with those expected using the empirical rule. What can you conclude about the generality of the empirical rule? Are any of the data classified as outliers by the MEAN ± 2(STANDARD DEVIATION) method?

```
1 | 000     Key: 1 | 5 = 1.5
1 |
1 | 555555555
1 |
1 |
2 | 00000000000000000000000000
2 |
2 | 5555555555555555555555555555555555555555555
2 |
2 |
3 | 000000000000000000000000
```

100 Means Computed from Samples of Size $n = 2$ from the Spinner Population

4. If you were to take averages of size n from the population represented by the spinner in Application 18, would the empirical rule work better when $n = 15$ or when $n = 2$? Why?

5. The batting averages of the National League batting champions from 1941–91 were given in Application 13. The mean and standard deviation of that set of data were $\bar{x} = .344$ and $s = 0.014$. What percentage of the data fall within ($\bar{x} - s$, $\bar{x} + s$)? Within ($\bar{x} - 2s, \bar{x} + 2s$)? Within ($\bar{x} - 3s, \bar{x} + 3s$)? Compare your results with the percentages predicted by the empirical rule. Does the empirical rule apply to these data? Why?

6. Take a random sample of size $n = 20$ from the population represented by the spinner in Application 18 and compute $\bar{x}$ and s. How many data elements fall within ($\bar{x} - s, \bar{x} + s$)? Within ($\bar{x} - 2s, \bar{x} + 2s$)? Within ($\bar{x} - 3s, \bar{x} + 3s$)? Compare your results with those predicted by the empirical rule. Is the empirical rule appropriate in this setting? Why? What can you conclude about the generality of the empirical rule? Are any of your data classified as outliers by the MEAN $\pm$ 2(STANDARD DEVIATION) method?

7. Thirty patients at the St. Cloud (Minnesota) Hospital had their temperatures taken immediately after major surgery. Their temperatures in degrees Fahrenheit were as follows:

$$93.9 \quad 95.0 \quad 94.4 \quad 95.7 \quad 95.2 \quad 95.0$$
$$95.4 \quad 94.5 \quad 95.1 \quad 95.7 \quad 95.0 \quad 94.2$$
$$95.2 \quad 96.9 \quad 95.6 \quad 92.5 \quad 92.6 \quad 93.7$$
$$94.6 \quad 95.0 \quad 96.4 \quad 95.0 \quad 96.5 \quad 93.7$$
$$94.3 \quad 96.7 \quad 95.2 \quad 95.7 \quad 95.9 \quad 94.7$$

Find $\bar{x}$ and s and make a stem-and-leaf plot for these data. Compare the numbers predicted by the empirical rule with the number of the data falling within the intervals ($\bar{x} - s, \bar{x} + s$), ($\bar{x} - 2s, \bar{x} + 2s$), and ($\bar{x} - 3s, \bar{x} + 3s$). Does the empirical rule apply to these data? Why? Are any of the data classified as outliers by the MEAN $\pm$ 2(STANDARD DEVIATION) method?

8. Give an example of a sample where the empirical rule gives poor estimates of the numbers of observations that fall in both ($\bar{x} - s, \bar{x} + s$) and ($\bar{x} - 2s, \bar{x} + 2s$).

9. Collect some data of your choice. For example, find the amount of time that each of your mathematics classmates takes to get to school or spends watching television each day. Find $\bar{x}$ and s for your data. Compare the numbers predicted by the empirical rule with the number of the data falling within the intervals $(\bar{x} - s, \bar{x} + s)$, $(\bar{x} - 2s, \bar{x} + 2s)$, and $(\bar{x} - 3s, \bar{x} + 3s)$. Does the empirical rule apply to these data? Why? Are any of the data classified as outliers by the MEAN $\pm$ 2(STANDARD DEVIATION) method?

Predicting the Variation in Sample Means

Suppose you obtain a set of sample means by repeatedly taking samples of size n from a population whose standard deviation (σ) can be found by using the data in an ideal sample. Is there a relationship between the sample standard deviation of the means ($s_{\bar{x}}$) you have generated, the standard deviation of the population, and the size of the samples—that is, can you find a relationship between $s_{\bar{x}}$, σ, and n?

A good place to begin looking for an answer to this question is with the 7 sets of 100 sample means that were obtained by repeatedly sampling the population represented by a fair die and that are listed on pages 69–72. The sample sizes used in computing the sample means and the sample standard deviation, $s_{\bar{x}}$, for each set of means are reproduced below. As you learned on p. 64, the population standard deviation is $\sigma = \sqrt{\frac{35}{12}} \approx 1.7078$

	$n = 2$	$n = 3$	$n = 4$	$n = 5$	$n = 10$	$n = 20$	$n = 30$
Sample Std. Dev. of the Means ($s_{\bar{x}}$)	1.232	0.937	0.876	0.704	0.518	0.399	0.312

Sample Standard Deviation for Each Set of Means

At first glance, there does not appear to be any relationship between σ and the seven values of $s_{\bar{x}}$ and n. There are two reasons for this: the relationship is more complicated than expected and is statistical rather than mathematical. By looking at some specific examples, the well-hidden pattern will become a lot easier to see. Notice the following:

when $n = 2$, $s_{\bar{x}} = 1.232 \approx 1.2076 = \dfrac{\sigma}{\sqrt{2}}$

when $n = 3$, $s_{\bar{x}} = 0.937 \approx 0.9860 = \dfrac{\sigma}{\sqrt{3}}$

and

when $n = 4$, $s_{\bar{x}} = 0.876 \approx 0.8539 = \dfrac{\sigma}{\sqrt{4}}$

If you were to continue in this fashion using the data in the table above, you would be led to conclude that $s_{\bar{x}} \approx \sigma/\sqrt{n}$ when means are obtained by repeatedly taking samples of size n from the fair die population. In Application 23, you will be given an opportunity to explore this statistical relationship when repeatedly sampling other populations; and you will discover that the following rule always works, provided it is possible to compute σ.

$$s_{\bar{x}} \approx \frac{\sigma}{\sqrt{n}}$$

The relationship $s_{\bar{x}} \approx \sigma/\sqrt{n}$ is useful for two reasons. Since $\sigma/\sqrt{n}$ decreases to 0 as n gets large, it provides a mathematical justification for the assertion that the variation in a set of sample means obtained by repeated sampling decreases as the sample size gets large. It also enables us to restate the empirical rule in a different and sometimes more useful form. Recall that one version of the empirical rule states that when samples of size n are repeatedly selected from a population and the mean of each sample is computed, approximately 68% of the means obtained will fall in ($\bar{x} - s_{\bar{x}}, \bar{x} + s_{\bar{x}}$), approximately 95% will fall in ($\bar{x} - 2s_{\bar{x}}, \bar{x} + 2s_{\bar{x}}$), and essentially all will be in ($\bar{x} - 3s_{\bar{x}}, \bar{x} + 3s_{\bar{x}}$), provided that a line plot of the means is roughly mound-shaped. These intervals estimate ($\mu - \sigma/\sqrt{n}, \mu + \sigma/\sqrt{n}$), ($\mu - 2\sigma/\sqrt{n}, \mu + 2\sigma/\sqrt{n}$), and ($\mu - 3\sigma/\sqrt{n}, \mu + 3\sigma/\sqrt{n}$), respectively. This is because $\bar{x}$ and $s_{\bar{x}}$ are good estimates of μ and $\sigma/\sqrt{n}$. These observations suggest a reformulation of the empirical rule—that is when random samples of size n are repeatedly selected from a population with a mean (μ) and standard deviation (σ), approximately 68% of the sample means will fall in ($\mu - \sigma/\sqrt{n}$, $\mu + \sigma/\sqrt{n}$), approximately 95% of the sample means will fall in ($\mu - 2\sigma/\sqrt{n}, \mu + 2\sigma/\sqrt{n}$), and essentially all will be in ($\mu - 3\sigma/\sqrt{n}, \mu + 3\sigma/\sqrt{n}$), provided that a line plot of an ideal sample from the population is mound-shaped. Another way of thinking of this is that if a single random sample of size n is selected from a population the sample mean ($\bar{x}$) is computed as follows:

$$P(\mu - \sigma/\sqrt{n} < \bar{x} < \mu + \sigma/\sqrt{n}) \approx .68$$

$$P(\mu - 2\sigma/\sqrt{n} < \bar{x} < \mu + 2\sigma/\sqrt{n}) \approx .95$$

and

$$P(\mu - 3\sigma/\sqrt{n} < \bar{x} < \mu + 3\sigma/\sqrt{n}) \approx 1.00$$

This is provided that a line plot of an ideal sample is mound-shaped. Here, for example, $P(\mu - \sigma/\sqrt{n} < \bar{x} < \mu + \sigma/\sqrt{n})$ is read "the probability that $\bar{x}$ is between $\mu - \sigma/\sqrt{n}$ and $\mu + \sigma/\sqrt{n}$." Your explorations in the next section begin with this important version of the empirical rule.

As an example of this new version of the empirical rule, think of an Aggravation player who wants to estimate the likelihood of averaging 4 or more per roll in 20 rolls of a fair die without using the method of simulation described earlier in this section. Letting $\bar{x}$ represent the mean number per roll over the next $n = 20$ rolls, we have the following:

$$.68 \approx P(\mu - \sigma/\sqrt{n} < \bar{x} < \mu + \sigma/\sqrt{n})$$

$$= P\left[3.5 - \sqrt{(35/12)}\,/\sqrt{20} < \bar{x} < 3.5 + \sqrt{(35/12)}\,/\sqrt{20}\right]$$

$$= P(3.1181 < \bar{x} < 3.8819)$$

$$.95 \approx P(\mu - 2\sigma/\sqrt{n} < \bar{x} < \mu + 2\sigma/\sqrt{n})$$

$$= P\left[3.5 - 2\sqrt{(35/12)}\,/\sqrt{20} < \bar{x} < 3.5 + 2\sqrt{(35/12)}\,/\sqrt{20}\right]$$

$$= P(2.7362 < \bar{x} < 4.2638)$$

and

$$1.00 \approx P(\mu - 3\sigma/\sqrt{n} < \bar{x} < \mu + 3\sigma/\sqrt{n})$$

$$= P\left[3.5 - 3\sqrt{(35/12)}\,/\sqrt{20} < \bar{x} < 3.5 + 3\sqrt{(35/12)}\,/\sqrt{20}\right]$$

$$= P(2.3544 < \bar{x} < 4.6456)$$

Thus, the Aggravation® player may conclude the following in 20 rolls of a fair die:

1. The probability of averaging at least 3.88 is about .16 (since 68% of the probability is between 3.11 and 3.88).

2. The probability of averaging at least 4.26 is about .025 (since 95% of the probability is between 2.74 and 4.26).

3. The probability of averaging at least 4.6456 is essentially 0.

These conclusions are valid because a line plot of an ideal sample is mound-shaped (line plots that are both symmetric and flat are considered mound-shaped).

Remark: You have now seen three versions of the empirical rule that apply to similar but somewhat different situations. They are summarized below to help you see how they are related and when they apply.

1. If samples of size n are repeatedly taken from a population and the mean of each sample computed, approximately 68% of the sample means will fall in ($\bar{\bar{x}} - s_{\bar{x}}, \bar{\bar{x}} + s_{\bar{x}}$), approximately 95% will fall in ($\bar{\bar{x}} - 2s_{\bar{x}}, \bar{\bar{x}} + 2s_{\bar{x}}$), and essentially all will fall in ($\bar{\bar{x}} - 3s_{\bar{x}}, \bar{\bar{x}} + 3s_{\bar{x}}$), provided that a line plot of the means is approximately mound-shaped (which is usually the case when working with sets of means).

2. If a single random sample of size n is selected from a population, approximately 68% of the data will fall in ($\bar{x} - s, \bar{x} + s$), approximately 95% of the data will fall in ($\bar{x} - 2s, \bar{x} + 2s$), and essentially all of the data will fall in ($\bar{x} - 3s, \bar{x} + 3s$), provided a line plot of the data is mound-shaped.

3. If a single random sample of size n is selected from a population with a mean (μ) and standard deviation (σ), the probability that $\bar{x}$ falls in ($\mu - \sigma/\sqrt{n}, \mu + \sigma/\sqrt{n}$) is approximately .68, the probability that $\bar{x}$ falls in ($\mu - 2\sigma/\sqrt{n}, \mu + 2\sigma/\sqrt{n}$) is approximately .95, and the probability that $\bar{x}$ falls in ($\mu - 3\sigma/\sqrt{n}, \mu + 3\sigma/\sqrt{n}$) is essentially 1.00, provided that a line plot of an ideal sample is mound-shaped.

Versions 2 and 3 of the empirical rule are most useful because we generally do not find ourselves in real-world situations that involve repeated sampling. By viewing the n elements in a single sample as means of samples of size 1, Version 2 is seen to be a special case of Version 1. Version 3 applies when we have the luxury of knowing a population's mean and standard deviation.

<hr>

Application 23

$s_{\bar{x}}$, $\sigma/\sqrt{n}$, and the Empirical Rule

1. Use the table on p. 84 to continue exploring the relationship between $s_{\bar{x}}$ and $\sigma/\sqrt{n}$ when the fair die population is repeatedly sampled and $n = 5, 10, 20,$ and 30. Describe the pattern that you see.

2. For each n ($n = 2, 3, 4, 5, 10, 20,$ and 30), 100 samples of size n were selected from the population represented by the table of random numbers, and the mean of each sample was computed. The sample standard deviation ($s_{\bar{x}}$), for each set of 100 means is given below. Use these data to explore and discuss the relationship between $s_{\bar{x}}$ and $\sigma/\sqrt{n}$.

$n = 2$	$n = 3$	$n = 4$	$n = 5$	$n = 10$	$n = 20$	$n = 30$
1.932	1.827	1.301	1.442	0.9265	0.5951	0.5372

3. In problems 2 and 3 of Application 20, you worked with means computed from samples of size $n = 2$ and $n = 3$ from the population represented by the spinner in Application 18. Use these two sets of sample means to explore and discuss the relationship between $s_{\bar{x}}$ and $\sigma/\sqrt{n}$.

4. For $n = 2, 3, 4, 5, 10, 20,$ and 30, 100 samples of size n were selected from the population represented by the spinner in Application 18, and the mean of each sample was computed. The sample standard deviation, $s_{\bar{x}}$, for each set of 100 means is given below. Use these data to explore and discuss the relationship between $s_{\bar{x}}$ and $\sigma/\sqrt{n}$.

$n = 2$	$n = 3$	$n = 4$	$n = 5$	$n = 10$	$n = 20$	$n = 30$
0.5143	0.4274	0.3428	0.3501	0.2645	0.1783	0.1399

5. Two hundred means are generated by repeatedly taking samples of size $n = 15$ from the population represented by the spinner in Application 18. The sample standard deviation of this set of means should be close to what number?

6. The standard deviation of an ideal sample of test scores in a certain very large mathematics class is 15. If you repeatedly took samples of size $n = 10$ and computed the mean of each sample, the sample standard deviation of the means ($s_{\bar{x}}$) should be close to what number? Suppose, further, that an ideal sample mean is 170. If 25 more people are to take the exam, what is the probability that their average score will be at least 173? At least 176? Will be

at most 167? Will be between 164 and 176? Will be between 164 and 173? What assumption(s) did you have to make in order to answer the last 5 questions in this problem?

7. Because it takes too long, an Aggravation® player does not want to use the method of simulation to estimate the likelihood of averaging 4 or more per roll in 40 rolls of a fair die. What can the player conclude using the empirical rule?

8. Christy, a member of the girl's swim team, works out regularly on the Nautilus equipment at the local YMCA during her off-season. The mean and standard deviation of an ideal sample of her workout times in minutes are 40.5 and 5.5, respectively. The average amount of time Christy will spend working out on her next 10 visits to the YMCA will fall between what numbers with probability about .68? With probability about .95? With probability essentially 1.00? What is the probability that over her next 20 visits to the YMCA Christy will average between 39.270 and 42.960 minutes working out? Between 38.040 and 44.190 minutes working out? At least 42.960 minutes working out? At most 39.270 minutes working out? What assumption(s) did you have to make to answer these questions?

9. Almost every day during the off-season, Ted, a member of the boy's basketball team, practices shooting 20 free throws. The mean and standard deviation of an ideal sample of the percentages of free throws that he makes are 85 and 12, respectively. The average percentage of free throws that Ted will make during the next 16 days will fall between what two numbers with probability about .68? With probability about .95? With probability essentially 1.00? What is the probability that over the next 9 days Ted will average between 77% and 93% of his free-throws? Between 73% and 89%? At most 77% of his free throws? At least 89% of his free throws? What assumption did you have to make to answer these questions? Is it reasonable to believe that this assumption is satisfied? Why?

10. A mathematics exam that all seniors are required to take before graduating is scaled so that an ideal sample will have a mean of 75 and a standard deviation of 5. If your school has $n = 200$ students who will take this exam and if they score like other students who have been required to take this exam in the past, the average score for this group of 200 students will fall in what interval with probability about .68? With probability about .95? What assumption did you make in answering these questions?

11. Sixty-four digits are to be randomly selected from the population represented by the random number table. The mean of these digits will fall in what interval with probability about .68? With probability about .95? With probability about 1.00? The mean of these digits will be at least what number with probability about .16? What assumption did you make in answering these questions? Is it reasonable to believe that this assumption is satisfied? Why?

12. The values for the sum of the dots showing when two standard (fair) dice are rolled are 2, 3, . . . , 12. An ideal sample from the population of all possible sums contains 36 elements. List them and find the mean and standard deviation of the population. If this pair of dice are rolled 10 times and the sum of the dots showing on each roll (of the pair) is recorded, the average (mean) of the 10 sums will fall between what numbers with probability about .68? With probability about

.95? With probability essentially 1.00? What is the probability that over the next 20 rolls of this pair of dice the average of the sums will be between 5.920 and 7.540? Between 7 and 8.080? More than 6.460? What assumption(s) did you have to make to answer these questions? Explain why you think those assumptions are satisfied.

Estimating Variation in a Population

(This section is optional; the remaining sections do not depend on this material.)

The *variance* of a population for which an ideal sample exists is defined as the square of the population's standard deviation and is therefore denoted σ^2. For example, using the formula on p. 64, the variance of the population represented by a fair die is $\sigma^2 = [\sqrt{35/12}]^2 = \frac{35}{12} \approx 2.917$. Because σ^2 is large (or small) when σ is large (or small), the population variance is frequently used as a measure of spread or variability. When a sample is not ideal, σ^2 may be estimated by the square of the sample standard deviation, s^2, which is called the *sample variance*. Notice that both σ^2 and s^2 are reported in square units. For example, if the population is the set of ages in years of secondary-school teachers in the United States, then the units for reporting both σ^2 and s^2 are (years)^2.

At the beginning of this section, we argued intuitively that where $x_1, x_2, \ldots, x_n$ are data in a sample size n, a good estimator of σ is as follows:

$$s = \sqrt{\frac{\sum_{i=1}^{n}(x_i - \bar{x})^2}{n-1}}$$

This fact has been used a substantial number of times to describe the variability in sets of sample means. Another possible estimator of σ is the following:

$$s' = \sqrt{\frac{\sum_{i=1}^{n}(x_i - \bar{x})^2}{n}}$$

This one is, perhaps, more natural since its computation involves taking an average; and the formula more closely resembles that for computing a population's standard deviation. Which statistic, s^2 or s'^2 is the better estimator of s^2? Which statistic, s or s', is the better estimator of σ?

A good way to find answers to these questions is to repeatedly sample populations where σ^2 is known. By observing the values of s^2 and s'^2 for each sample, you may be able to see which of s^2 and s'^2 gives better estimates of σ^2 and, consequently, which of s and s' gives better estimates of σ.

Let's begin with data from 10 samples of size $n = 6$ from the population represented by a fair die. Tallies of the numbers showing on the die and the values of $\bar{x}$, s^2, and s'^2 for each sample are given below.

Out-come	Sample									
	1	2	3	4	5	6	7	8	9	10
1	I		I	I	I I I	I I		I		I I
2		I	I	I I	I	I		I	I I	
3	I I		I	I I					I	I I
4	I	I	I			I I	++++	I	I	I
5	I	I			I	I		I I	I	
6	I	I I I	I I	I	I		I	I	I	I
$\bar{x}$	3.67	4.83	3.67	2.83	2.67	2.83	4.33	3.83	3.66	3.00
s^2	3.07	2.57	4.27	2.97	5.07	2.97	0.67	3.77	2.67	3.60
s'^2	2.56	2.14	3.56	2.47	4.22	2.47	0.56	3.14	2.22	3.00

Ten Samples of Size $n = 6$ from the Population Represented by a Fair Die

Upon comparing s^2 and s'^2 for these sets of data, you might notice that s'^2 is always smaller than s^2. This is not surprising because $s'^2 = [(n - 1)/n\,]s^2$. Indeed, because $n = 6$, each s'^2 is $5/6$ of the corresponding s^2 value. What is less obvious but more crucial is that s^2 is generally a little closer to $\sigma^2 = 2.917$ than is s'^2 and that the average of the 10 s'^2 is 2.63 while the average of all the 10 s^2 is 3.16, that is, for these sets of data, s^2 seems to provide a slightly better estimate of σ^2 than does s'^2. To help you see that this is generally the case, it is necessary to examine how the values of s^2 and s'^2 are distributed when populations with different shapes are repeatedly sampled. Of course, such a project is too lengthy to include here; but, by examining the following plots and data, you should get a good idea of what happens. Let's begin by looking below at comparative box plots of the s^2 and s'^2 values that we obtained from each of 100 samples of size n from the population represented by a fair die when $n = 2, 3, 4, 5, 10, 20,$ and 30. Box plots of the 7 sets of 100 s'^2 values appear first, followed by box plots of the 7 sets of 100 s'^2 values. Each set of plots is arranged sequentially downward, beginning with the box plot for $n = 2$ at the top and ending with the box plot for $n = 30$ at the bottom. In these and subsequent box plots, the asterisks (*) indicate data that fall outside the interval (sample lower quartile – 1.5(sample interquartile range), sample upper quartile + 1.5(sample interquartile range)). Do you see any pattern(s)?

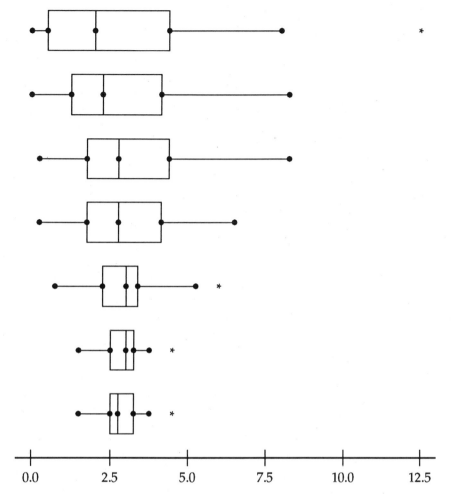

Box Plots of Sets of s² Values Obtained by Taking Samples of Size n = 2, 3, 4, 5, 10, 20, and 30 from the Population Represented by a Fair Die

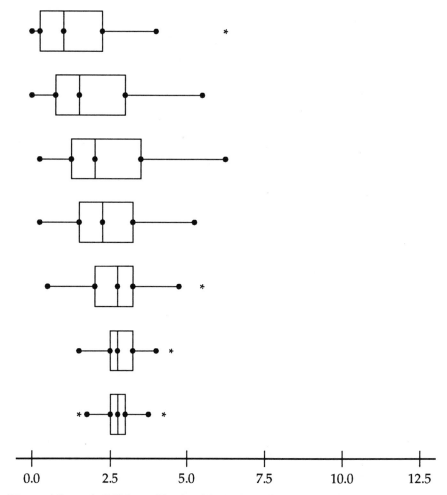

Box Plots of Sets of s'^2 Values Obtained by Taking Samples of Size $n = 2, 3, 4, 5, 10, 20,$ and 30 from the Population Represented by a Fair Die

The mean of each set of 100 s^2 and s'^2 is given in the table below for each n. What pattern(s) do you see?

	$n = 2$	$n = 3$	$n = 4$	$n = 5$	$n = 10$	$n = 20$	$n = 30$
Average of 100 s^2s	2.735	2.893	3.112	3.020	2.924	2.938	2.871
Average of 100 s'^2s	1.367	1.929	2.334	2.416	2.632	2.791	2.776

Samples from the Population Represented by a Fair Die

In a similar fashion, we took 100 samples of size n from the populations represented by the random number table and the spinner in Application 18 and computed s^2 and s'^2 for each sample when $n = 2, 3, 4, 5, 10, 20,$ and 30. Comparative box plots like those above appear below along with tables showing how the means of the s^2s and s'^2s change as n gets large when repeatedly sampling these two populations. The 0s indicate data that falls outside the interval (sample lower quartile − 3(sample interquartile range), sample upper quartile + 3(sample interquartile range)). Do the patterns you observed when sampling from the population represented by a fair die hold when sampling from these two other populations? What effect does sampling from a skewed population seem to have? In answering these questions, recall that $\sigma^2 = 8.25$ for the population represented by the table of random numbers and $\sigma^2 = 5/9$ for the population represented by the spinner.

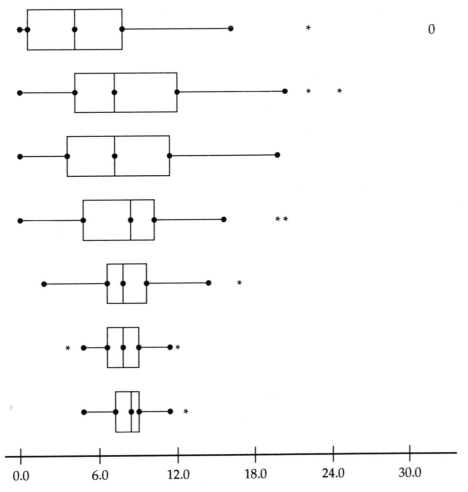

Box Plots of Sets of s^2 Values Obtained by Taking Samples of Size $n = 2, 3, 4, 5, 10, 20,$ and 30 from the Population Represented by the Table of Random Numbers

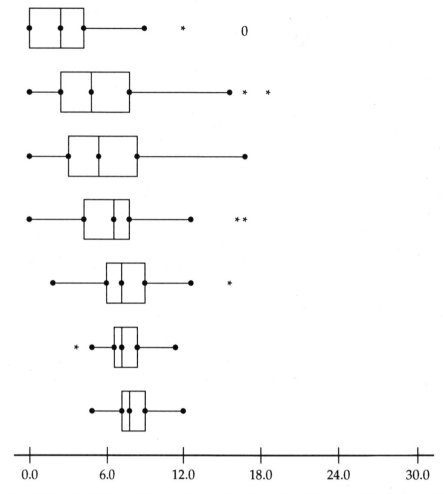

Box Plots of Sets of s'^2 Values Obtained by taking Samples of Size $n =2, 3, 4, 5, 10, 20,$ and 30 from the Population Represented by the Table of Random Numbers

	$n = 2$	$n = 3$	$n = 4$	$n = 5$	$n = 10$	$n = 20$	$n = 30$
Average of 100 s^2s	7.540	8.240	7.501	7.950	7.999	8.071	8.244
Average of 100 s'^2s	3.770	5.493	5.626	6.360	7.199	7.667	7.969

Samples from the Population Represented by the Table of Random Numbers

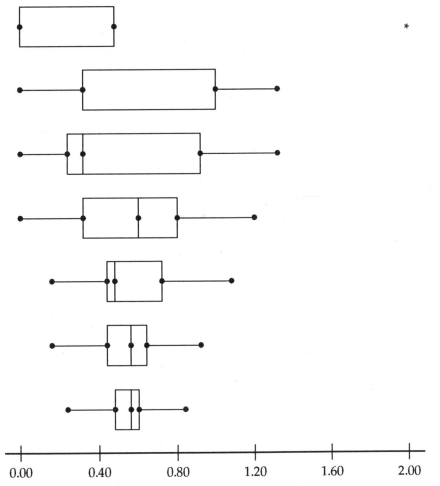

Box Plots of Sets of s^2 Values Obtained by Taking Samples of Size n = 2, 3, 4, 5, 10, 20, and 30 from the Population Represented by the Spinner in Application 18

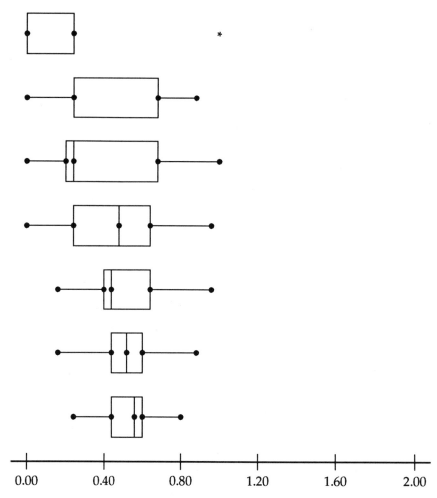

Box Plots of Sets of s'^2 Values Obtained by Taking Samples of Size $n = 2, 3, 4, 5, 10, 20,$ and 30 from the Population Represented by the Spinner in Application 18

	$n = 2$	$n = 3$	$n = 4$	$n = 5$	$n = 10$	$n = 20$	$n = 30$
Average of 100 s^2s	.5300	.5600	.5192	.5660	.5626	.5467	.5490
Average of 100 s'^2s	.2650	.3733	.3894	.4528	.5063	.5194	.5307

Samples from the Population Represented by the Spinner in Application 18

Discussion Questions

1. How does the shape of the distribution of s^2 change as n gets large when samples are repeatedly taken from the population represented by a fair die? The population represented by the table of random numbers? The population represented by the spinner?

2. How are the shapes of the distributions of s^2 and s'^2 related as n gets large when sampling from each of the three populations?

3. How does the mean of the distribution of s^2 change as n gets large when sampling from each of the three populations?

4. How are the means of the distributions of s^2 and s'^2 related as n gets large when sampling from each of the three populations?

5. Which statistic, s^2 or s'^2, do you think is most likely to give the best estimate of a population's variance? Why? Which statistic, s or s' is most likely to give the best estimate of a population's standard deviation? Why?

Application 24

How Do You Get Good Data?

Many problems we would like to solve by collecting data seem easy until we actually begin to collect the data. The following activity is designed to have you think carefully about the measurement process. How can good data be obtained in the first place? That is a key question to be asked of all quantitative investigations.

Instructions

Working in groups, think carefully about how to design a data-collection scheme for each of the following situations:

1. Measuring the height and pulse (heart rate) for each member of the class.

2. Determining how fast a track team member and you run the 440.

3. Determining the height of a tall tree.

4. Determining the distance from home to school by using the odometer on the family car.

5. Comparing the prices of name-brand jeans in two retail outlets in your town.

Analysis

Each group should choose one of the above situations and actually carry out the data collection. The resulting data should be plotted and summarized for a presentation to the remainder of the class.

Discussion

Each group should discuss the following within the group and then with the class as a whole.

1. What difficulties did we have in collecting the data?

2. How could we improve the experiment if we were to conduct it again?

Patterns That Arise in Repeated Sampling—Summary

When it is too difficult, too costly, or impossible to list all of the data in a population, a subset of the population, called a random sample, is selected in such a way that the data obtained are representative of the population. A sample that produces exactly the same data in exactly the same proportions as the population, is called an ideal sample. Unfortunately, most samples are not ideal. The mean, median, standard deviation, and variance of a sample (represented by $\bar{x}$, m, s, and s^2, respectively) are called statistics. These statistics are frequently used to estimate and make inferences about the mean, median, standard deviation, and variance of the population (represented by μ, M, σ, and σ^2, respectively). If an element of a sample falls outside either of the intervals, $(\bar{x} - 2s, \bar{x} + 2s)$ or ((sample lower quartile – 1.5(sample interquartile range), sample upper quartile + 1.5(sample interquartile range)), it is considered unusual and may be called an outlier.

As the sample size gets larger, line plots of sample means become more mound-shaped and less variable, while staying centered at the population mean regardless of the shape of the population. This explains why the sample mean is ordinarily used to estimate and make inferences about the population mean: as the sample size gets larger, it becomes more likely that a sample mean will be close to the population mean.

The empirical rule explains how to assess variability in a set of data. One version of this rule says that if a line plot of the data is mound-shaped then approximately 68% of the data will fall in the interval $(\bar{x} - s, \bar{x} + s)$, approximately 95% of the data will fall in $(\bar{x} - 2s, \bar{x} + 2s)$, and essentially all (100%) will fall in $(\bar{x} - 3s, \bar{x} + 3s)$. Another version of the empirical rule states that if $\bar{x}$ is the mean of a sample of size n from a population with a mean (μ) and standard deviation (σ), then $\bar{x}$ falls in $(\mu - \sigma/\sqrt{n}, \mu + \sigma/\sqrt{n})$ with probability approximately .68, $\bar{x}$ falls in $(\mu - 2\sigma/\sqrt{n}, \mu + 2\sigma/\sqrt{n})$ with probability approximately .95, and $\bar{x}$ falls in $(\mu - 3\sigma/\sqrt{n}, \mu + 3\sigma/\sqrt{n})$ with probability approximately 1.00, provided that a line plot of an ideal sample is mound-shaped.

The statistics s^2 and $s'^2 = [(n - 1) / n]s^2$ may be used to estimate a population's variance, σ^2. When the sample size, n, is small, the numerical values of these two statistics can be quite different, while for large n they produce very similar values. This is because $(n - 1) / n$ increases to 1 as n gets larger. The sampling distributions of both s^2 and s'^2 are noticeably skewed to the right when n is small and become more mound-shaped, less variable, and more like each other as the sample size gets larger, regardless of the shape of the population. Since the center of the distribution of s^2 is always σ^2 while the center of the distribution of s'^2 is always less than σ^2 (approaching σ^2 as n gets larger), s^2 is said to be an unbiased estimate of σ^2 while s'^2 is said to be biased. Because s^2 is more likely than s'^2 to be close to σ^2 and, consequently, s is more likely than s' to be close to σ, s^2 and s are usually used to estimate and make inferences about σ^2 and σ.

III. ESTIMATING AN UNKNOWN POPULATION MEAN

Likely vs. Unlikely Sample Means

Scores on the verbal portion of the SAT are scaled so that an ideal sample will have a mean of approximately 500 and a standard deviation of approximately 100. (The scores can range from 200 to 800.) For a particular test given across the nation, the 500 can be thought of as the mean of all the scores (the population mean, μ), and the 100 can be thought of as the standard deviation of all the scores (the population standard deviation, σ). Suppose that your school has $n = 25$ students taking this particular test. What can we say, *before* the test is taken, about possible values of the mean verbal score ($\bar{x}$) of the 25 students?

We know the following from Section II:

$$\mu \pm 2\frac{\sigma}{\sqrt{n}} = 500 \pm 2\frac{100}{\sqrt{25}}$$

$$= 500 \pm 40$$

$$= 460 \text{ to } 540$$

This interval will contain about 95% of the possible sample means for random samples of 25 scores. Therefore, if students from your school behave like a typical sample of students from around the country, it is quite *likely* that the mean score of the 25 students will be between 460 and 540. It is *unlikely* that the mean score for the 25 students would be, say, above 550 or below 425. For purposes of this discussion, we will designate the sample means between 460 and 540 as *likely* to occur and those either above 540 or below 460 as *unlikely* to occur.

Suppose that the 25 students from your school take the SAT and the mean verbal score turns out to be 475. Should the administrators of your school begin to make changes in the curriculum because your school appears to be below average? Probably not, since the 475 scored by your students is within the *likely* range of means for samples of this size from a population with mean 500. In other words, these 25 students do seem to behave like any typical sample of 25 students from across the country.

Suppose that the 25 students from your school take the SAT and the mean verbal score is 550. Is your school above average? Now, 550 is outside the range of likely mean values when sampling from a population with a mean of 500 and a standard deviation of 100. Therefore, something appears to be "different" about this sample. One of two explanations is possible. First, students at your school may still mirror the national picture, but the luck of the draw produced 25 very good test-takers for this particular test. Second, students at your school may actually be better than a typical selection of students from across the country! Since the first explanation involves an event that seldom occurs, we might lean toward the second explanation. We must at least consider the possibility that your school would consistently produce a mean score greater than 500, a possibility that could be monitored in future tests.

Let's now look at an example in which we must analyze an actual measurement process. Twenty students were asked to "measure" the length of a piece of string by looking at it and guessing the length to the nearest inch (this is a crude process, but it will illustrate a point). The 20 measurements (in inches) are given below:

```
1 | 8
2 | 0  2  4  4
2 | 5  5  5  6  8  9  9
3 | 0  0  0  1  2  2  4
3 | 6
```

It is expected that some students will guess on the high side and some will guess on the low side, so that the average (mean) guessed length should be fairly close to the true length of the string, which is known by the teacher to be 27 inches. How close will the sample mean of the 20 measurements be to μ? By comparing $\bar{x} = 27.5$ inches for this sample with $\mu = 27$, we see that the average guessed length seems to be pretty close to the actual length. But how close is it? If we asked several different groups of 20 students each to guess the length of the string, would the means of the guesses for these other groups tend to be closer than, as close as, or farther away than the mean of the first group? From earlier discussions, we know that $\mu \pm 2\sigma/\sqrt{n}$ will contain about 95% of the possible sample means. A problem with using this interval as a measure of closeness is that the population standard deviation (σ) is unknown. It may be estimated, though, by the sample standard deviation (s) calculated from the observed sample of 20 responses (hopefully random) from the original measurement process. This turns out to be $s = 4.66$ inches and the interval can be calculated as follows:

$$\mu \pm 2 \frac{s}{\sqrt{n}}$$

$$= 27 \pm 2 \frac{4.66}{\sqrt{20}}$$

$$= 27 \pm 2.08$$

This is the same as (24.92, 29.08). Note that the one $\bar{x}$ that we did observe falls inside this interval. For randomly obtained measurements on guessed lengths of this piece of string, approximately 95% of the sample means for samples of size 20 should lie between 24.92 and 29.08 inches.

A second sample of $n = 20$ measurements or guesses at the length of the string was taken from a different group of students. The data, shown below, have a mean of $\bar{x} = 28.3$ and a standard deviation of $s = 4.88$.

```
1 | 8
2 | 1   3   4
2 | 5   5   5   6   8   8
3 | 0   0   0   1   2   2   2   4
3 | 6   6
```

Note that, as in the first case, this sample mean is also between 24.92 and 29.08. On comparing the two sample standard deviations, we see that they are close. This indicates that either one of the two sample standard deviations may be a good approximation to σ, and the interval $\mu \pm 2s/\sqrt{n}$ will not change much if we use the s from the second sample. In fact, the interval becomes (24.82, 29.18), and both observed sample means are still within it.

Suppose that we took a third sample of $n = 20$ measurements on the string length from yet another group of 20 students and suppose that the sample mean turned out to be 30.10 inches. This is not in the *likely* set of outcomes for means of measurements from this process! Why? Something seems to have *biased* these measurements toward larger values. Perhaps someone mentioned a yard stick or meter stick. Perhaps someone compared the length of the string to the length of his arm. Perhaps someone mentioned a particularly large guess aloud and it influenced the others. Perhaps we were just unlucky in this sample. At any rate, the result is different from what we now expect. It is *unlikely*—and this may merit some further investigation. (This situation once happened to one of the authors. Upon investigation, one student checked her notes and admitted that she reported the wrong number by mistake, thus throwing off the entire sample mean.)

102

Suppose that we now combine the two sets of 20 measurements given above into one set of 40 measurements, as shown below:

```
1 | 8  8
2 | 0  1  2  3  4  4  4
2 | 5  5  5  5  5  5  6  6   8   8   8
3 | 0  0  0  0  0  0  1  1   2   2   2
3 | 6  6  6
```

For the combined data, $\bar{x} = 27.90$ and $s = 4.73$. Also look at the following:

$$\mu \pm 2 \frac{\sigma}{\sqrt{n}} =$$

$$27 \pm 2 \frac{4.73}{\sqrt{40}}$$

This yields 27 ± 1.50 inches, or $(25.5, 28.5)$. Notice that the estimated interval of likely sample means for samples of size 40 is much shorter than corresponding intervals for samples of size 20, even though the s for the larger sample is about the same as the s values for the smaller samples. What we have observed is an important general principle described in Section II; namely, that averages of random samples tend to become closer to the true mean as the sample size increases.

Application 25

1. A movie theater was known to average 200 paid admissions per weekend day (Friday, Saturday, Sunday) during last year. A sample of $n = 16$ weekend days for this year is available. The following assume $n = 16$.

   a. Suppose that $\bar{x} = 205$ and $s = 12$ for the sample. Would you say that attendance at the theater is improving? Why or why not?

   b. Suppose that $\bar{x} = 210$ and $s = 12$ for the sample. Would you now say that attendance appears to be improving?

   c. Suppose $\bar{x} = 210$ and $s = 24$ for another sample. Would you now say that attendance appears to be improving?

2. A manufacturer of 12-volt automobile batteries advertised that batteries of a certain type were specified to weigh 69 pounds (weight of a battery is an important quality measurement because it is related to the amount of lead in the battery plates). A purchaser of large numbers of these batteries (actually used in golf carts) decided to conduct a quality control check. The purchaser randomly selected ten batteries from a recent purchase and found the following weights (in pounds):

$$67, 64, 68, 65, 64, 66, 68, 65, 66, 69$$

Do you think this purchaser's shipment of batteries has a true average weight of 69 pounds? Justify your answer statistically.

3. Inventory audits of a firm require that the auditor compare the value of items listed on the firm's books (book value) with the true market value of those same items (audit value), for a random sample of items. Ten items were sampled from an office supply firm's stock room, with the following results on audit vs. book values (figures in dollars):

Item	Audit Value, y_i	Book Value, x_i	d_i
1	9	10	−1
2	14	12	+2
3	7	8	−1
4	29	26	+3
5	45	47	−2
6	109	112	−3
7	40	36	+4
8	238	240	−2
9	60	59	+1
10	170	167	+3

If the firm is doing a good job in keeping its books up to date, the average *difference* between audit and book values, for all items in stock, should be zero. Does this seem to be the case for the firm in question? Justify your answer statistically.

4. Your instructor has measured the area of a rectangular table top in your classroom with a meter stick. This is assumed to be an accurate measurement, in square centimeters.

   a. Group A is given a 15-centimeter ruler. Using this ruler, have each member of the group measure the area of the table top. Compute $\bar{x}$ and s for these measurements. How close should your sample average be to the "true" area? Obtain the true value from the teacher and see if the Group A mean is within the likely range.

   b. Group B is given a stick known to be 10 centimeters long but with no markings on it. Each member of the group measures the area of the table top with this stick. Compute $\bar{x}$ and s for the sample measurements. How close should the sample average be to the true area? Obtain the true value from the teacher, and see if the Group B sample mean is within the likely range for *measurements of this type*.

   c. Which is more accurate, Group A's measurements or Group B's measurements? Could the method used by Group B ever produce as accurate a result as that produced by Group A? If so, how could this be done?

5. United States minted copper-zinc pennies are designed to weigh 2.51 grams. Measure the weight of ten pennies, weighing each one separately.

a. Do you think the government is meeting this standard? Why or why not?

b. Would it be better if you weighed 20 pennies? Why or why not?

6. Think of a scheduled event that is a regular part of your life and that is supposed to occur at a fixed time (for example, you may plan to arrive at school at 7:55 A.M. each day; practice for a sports team may be scheduled to begin at 3:00 P.M.; and dinner may be scheduled at 6:00 P.M. during weekdays). Now, measure the time that this event *actually* takes place over the next ten days for which it is scheduled. The objective is to assess whether or not the event is tending to "slip" from its scheduled time. We can make this assessment by recording the differences between the observed times and the scheduled time: for example, if you arrive at school at 7:53, record 7:53 – 7:55 = –2 minutes; if you arrive at 8:00, record 8:00 – 7:55 = +5 minutes. If everything is operating well over the long run, the average difference should be close to zero. Calculate the differences for your chosen event. Calculate the standard deviation of these differences. Does it look like the schedule is being maintained? Justify your answer statistically.

Confidence Interval Estimate of a Mean

For each example discussed above, the population mean was either known exactly or a reasonably good guess was available. Questions then dealt with how close the sample mean was to the "true" value of the population mean. Now, we will build up to making statements about population means when nothing is known besides the information in a single sample. First, however, we will discuss another situation in which the population means are known.

From 1979–81 there was a major emphasis in the United States toward improving air quality. Data are available in the *Statistical Abstract of the U.S.* (1984 edition) on the annual number of days of poor air quality for major cities in the country. These data show that the mean number of days with poor air quality were as follows:

1979	98.0
1980	83.6
1981	64.9

The standard deviation for each year is around 60. We see that, on the average, much improvement was made.

Next, we will study how means of samples from $n = 10$ cities perform as estimators of the population means given above. One hundred samples, each of size $n = 10$, were taken from the data for each year. Line plots of the sample means are shown following.

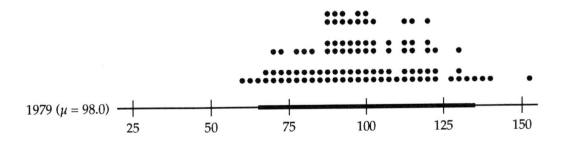

1979 ($\mu = 98.0$)

25   50   75   100   125   150

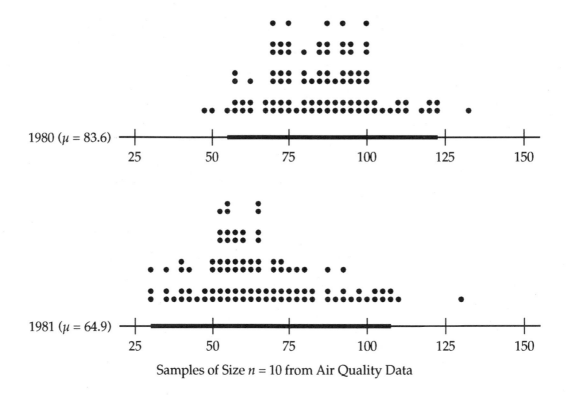

Samples of Size $n = 10$ from Air Quality Data

Note the shape of these distributions, which we should have anticipated from our discussions in Section II.

We now want to take the middle 95% of the sample mean values from each set as the likely ones. Since there are 100 means in each set, the closest that we can come to this in a symmetric way is to take the two smallest and two largest values off each set (leaving 96% in the middle). Thus, we mark the middle 96% to be those from the third smallest to third largest observed sample means, inclusively (there actually are no ties in these extreme positions even though the dots line up because of the scale).

The following table shows how the observed middle 96% intervals compare with the $\mu \pm 2(\sigma/\sqrt{n})$ intervals that the empirical rule suggests should cut off the middle 95%. The observed middle 96% intervals are marked on each line plot, as well. Recall that $\sigma = 60$ in all years and that the sample size is 10.

Year	Observed Middle 96%	$\mu \pm 2(\sigma/\sqrt{n})$
1979	(64.0, 136.7)	(60.0, 136.0)
1980	(54.4, 122.6)	(45.6, 121.6)
1981	(31.0, 107.0)	(26.9, 102.9)

Note that the agreement between observation and theory is good. The disagreement on the low side is partially due to the fact that the original data sets have many small values and few large ones (in other words, the data sets are not symmetric).

We took another sample of $n = 10$ cities from one of the years and found the mean number of poor air quality days to be 73.2. From which year was the new sample taken? On thinking about this, we might reason that since 73.2 is inside the likely range for all years, we cannot tell. And that seems to be the best conclusion (we can see this by locating 73.2 on the horizontal scale of the line plots and drawing a vertical line, which will intersect all three "middle 96% lines").

A secondary "mystery sample" of ten cities gave the mean number of days as 53.1. Using the same reasoning, we see that a vertical line from 53.1 on the line plots intersects only the "middle 96%" line of 1981—therefore, we can reasonably rule out the other two years. Choosing 1981 for this sample's year is, in fact, the correct choice.

We have been reasoning from the sample data in order to determine which populations could have produced these data. We decided to keep any populations for which the sample mean was in the *likely* range and to discard the others. This turns out to be an appropriate way to make statistical decisions. Although the process does not guarantee a correct decision in every case, in the long run it is far better than guessing. We will now look at generalizations of this procedure.

Suppose that we want to estimate the average weekly allowance (μ) for all students in your school. Both the average allowance (μ) and the standard deviation of allowances (σ) are unknown. But, the interval $\mu \pm 2\sigma/\sqrt{n}$ contains the *likely* sample means for random samples of n students. Suppose that we select a random sample of $n = 25$ students from the school and suppose (for the moment) that the population standard deviation (σ), though unknown, is assumed to be $5. Then $\mu \pm 2\sigma/\sqrt{n}$ yields the following:

$$\mu \pm 2 \, \frac{5}{\sqrt{25}}$$

This is $\mu \pm 2$ and is the interval of likely sample means (with measurements in dollars). Theoretically, μ can be any of a fairly large set of non-negative real numbers. Thus, there are many possible intervals containing the likely sample means, that is, for $\mu = 3$ the interval is (1, 5), for $\mu = 6$ the interval is (4, 8), for $\mu = 7$ the interval is (5, 9), and so on. We show these intervals on the following graph (the horizontal lines showing the likely 95% of means are similar to the solid lines on the line plot).

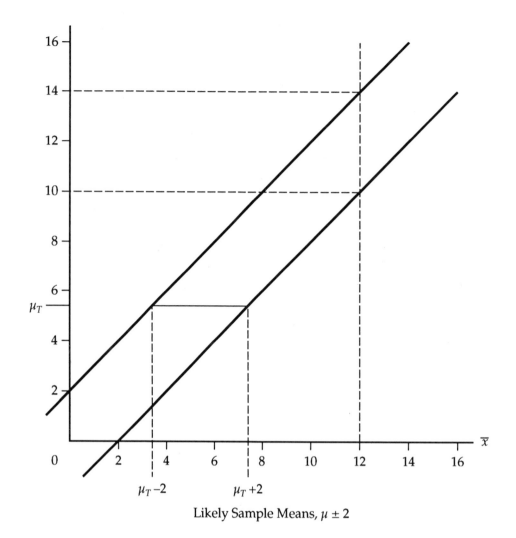

Likely Sample Means, $\mu \pm 2$

For any population mean (μ) found on the vertical axis, the interval of likely sample-mean ($\bar{x}$) values are those on the horizontal axis below the horizontal line segment between the angled lines. Thus, for a typical population mean, say μ_T, the likely sample means fall in the interval $\mu_T - 2$ to $\mu_T + 2$.

Now, suppose a sample of $n = 25$ students gave $\bar{x} = 12.00$ dollars as the average weekly allowance. What values of the population mean (μ) would have a sample mean $\bar{x} = 12$ inside the sets of likely sample means (for $n = 25$)? These population mean (μ) values can be determined by drawing a vertical line from $\bar{x} = 12$ on the graph. Such a line intersects the lower angled line at $\mu = 10$ and the upper angled line at $\mu = 14$. Thus, any population mean (μ) between 10 and 14 would have $\bar{x} = 12$ inside its set of likely sample means. To convince yourself of this, go back to the vertical axis of population-mean μ-values, choose some values between 10 and 14, and check to see if $\bar{x} = 12$ is, indeed, inside the interval of likely sample means.

We can now say that the possible population means for which $\bar{x} = 12$ is a likely sample mean consist of those values of population mean (μ) between 10 and 14. This interval (10, 14) is a 95% confidence interval estimate of the population mean (μ), the true (unknown) mean weekly allowance for students in your school. Notice that the length of this interval (four units in this case) is the vertical distance between the two angled lines on the graph. Since the lines are at 45°, the vertical distance between the two angled lines is the same as the horizontal distance between them. (This result comes about since the population mean (μ) and sample mean ($\bar{x}$) are measured on the same scale.) Since the horizontal distance between the angled lines was the following:

$$\mu - 2\,\frac{\sigma}{\sqrt{n}} \text{ to } \mu + 2\,\frac{\sigma}{\sqrt{n}}$$

The vertical distance is as follows:

$$\bar{x} - 2\frac{\sigma}{\sqrt{n}} \text{ to } \bar{x} + 2\frac{\sigma}{\sqrt{n}}$$

Thus, we have a simple way to write down the 95% confidence interval estimate of the population mean (μ):

$$\bar{x} \pm 2\frac{\sigma}{\sqrt{n}}$$

The argument used above in constructing a confidence interval does not depend upon the particular values of the population standard deviation (σ) or the sample size (n). Suppose that, in the estimation of average weekly allowance, the population standard deviation (σ) was 7 and the sample size (n) was 100. Then, $\mu \pm 2\sigma/\sqrt{n}$ becomes $\mu \pm 2(7/\sqrt{100})$, or $\mu \pm 1.4$. The likely sample means ($\bar{x}$'s) for a particular population mean (μ), say μ_T, are those within the horizontal interval between the angled lines in the following graph.

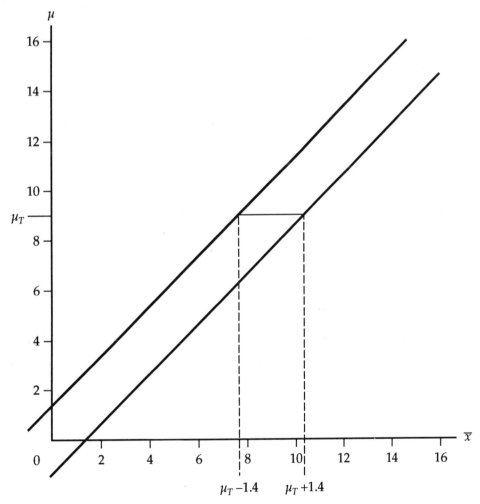

Likely Sample Means, $\mu \pm 1.4$

For a given observed sample mean, say $\bar{x} = 9$, the vertical distance between the angled lines goes from $9 - 1.4$ to $9 + 1.4$, or 7.6 to 10.4. This interval is the 95% confidence interval estimate of the population mean (μ), the true average weekly allowance for all students in the school, for this case. Again, the confidence interval turns out to be the following:

$$\bar{x} \pm 2 \frac{\sigma}{\sqrt{n}}$$

This rule will work no matter what values of the population standard deviation (σ) and the sample size (n) are chosen, but n should be at least 20 in order for the method to work well.

There is still one problem. The form of the confidence interval, $\bar{x} \pm 2\frac{\sigma}{\sqrt{n}}$, assumes that we know the population standard deviation (σ), which, generally, will be unknown. What can we do then? We can estimate the population standard deviation (σ) by the sample standard deviation (s), after the sample data are collected. For example, suppose $n = 25$ students from your school were sampled and asked the amount of their weekly allowance. The 25 stated amounts have a mean of $\bar{x} = 11.50$ and a standard deviation of $s = 4.30$ (measurements in dollars). What is the 95% confidence interval estimate of the true mean weekly allowance (μ) for all students in your school? We can now approximate $2\frac{\sigma}{\sqrt{n}}$ by substituting the sample standard deviation (s) for the population standard deviation (σ) to obtain the following:

$$\bar{x} \pm 2 \frac{s}{\sqrt{n}}$$
$$= 11.50 \pm 2 \frac{4.30}{\sqrt{25}}$$

$$= 11.50 \pm 1.72$$

$$= 9.78 \text{ to } 13.22$$

We are estimating that for samples of size $n = 25$, the possible population means for which $\bar{x} = 11.50$ is a likely sample mean are those between 9.78 and 13.22.

Application 26

1. A sample of 15 two-bedroom, unfurnished apartments in the Gainesville, Florida, area (spring, 1992) had monthly rentals (in dollars) as given below:

375	345	429
450	455	379
381	325	350
335	235	395
349	325	320

Estimate the average monthly rental for all apartments of this type in the Gainesville area.

2. A sample of ads for domestic used cars in the Gainesville area was taken from a newspaper. The years of the cars (with the 19s suppressed) are as follows:

83	85	89	88	86	83	84	76	74	83	86	78	91
74	80	87	84	80	89	85	78	87	86	84	89	89
76	86	85	85	68	69	86	80	79	83	84	72	78
81												

Construct a confidence interval estimate of the mean year for all domestic used cars on sale in the Gainesville area. Do you think the sample of newspaper ads forms a random sample of all used cars on sale in the area?

3. For a sample of used car advertisements for foreign cars (in the same newspaper) the years were as follows:

88	89	88	88	85	84	91	80	85	89	91	84	88
89	87	87	87	86	85	82	87	87	85	83	68	90
90	87	87	85	86	90	88	83	90	83	76	86	85
79												

Construct a confidence interval estimate of the mean year for all foreign used cars on sale in the Gainesville area.

4. It is commonly assumed that foreign cars are of higher quality than domestic cars. The data in applications 2 and 3 may not appear to support this assumption. Explain. You may want to use line plots or box plots to aid your comparison.)

5. A large group of rabbits is being used in a nutrition study. A prestudy weight is recorded for each rabbit. After two months, the experimenter wants to obtain a rough approximation of the average weight gain of the rabbits. She selects $n = 10$ rabbits at random and weighs them. The original weights and current weights are presented in the accompanying table. Estimate the average weight gain for the entire group of rabbits.

Rabbit	Original Weight	Current Weight
1	3.2	4.1
2	3.0	4.0
3	2.9	4.1
4	2.8	3.9
5	2.8	3.7
6	3.1	4.1
7	3.0	4.2
8	3.2	4.1
9	2.9	3.9
10	2.8	3.8

Repeated Confidence Intervals

Shown below is the relative frequency distribution of a large set of examination scores. The scores are percentages out of 100. Notice that in this examination many students are doing well and many are doing poorly. There is a large number of scores between 20% and 30% and another large number between 80% and 90%. The mean of all scores is $\mu = 52.575$.

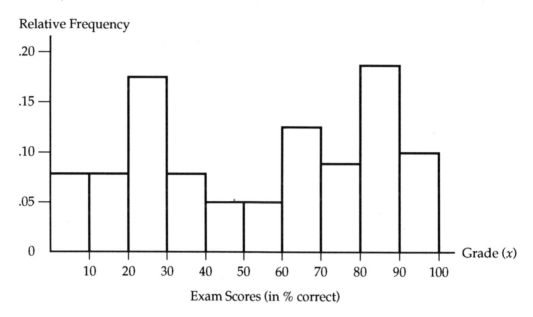

To illustrate the behavior of 95%-confidence-interval estimates of the population mean (μ), samples of size $n = 20$ are drawn from this set of scores. The population of scores remains the same for each sampling experiment—that is, each sample of scores is replaced (put back into the population) before the next sample of $n = 20$ scores is drawn. This process is repeated 50 times, producing the 50 confidence interval estimates of the population mean (μ) shown on the table that follows. The lines above the real number line indicate the length and position of each confidence interval.

It is important to note that 4 of the 50 confidence intervals *do not* overlap the true value of the population mean (μ)—that is, 4 of 50, or $\frac{4}{50}$, or 8% of the intervals, in repeated sampling, fail to enclose the true population mean (μ). In other words, 92% of the intervals, in repeated sampling, do contain the true population mean (μ). This 92% is remarkably close to the 95% that we used to define the *likely* sample means when we began this chapter. Now, we see another interpretation of that 95%. The method of constructing 95% confidence intervals is such that approximately 95% of intervals constructed, in repeated sampling, should enclose the true population mean, (μ). What do we mean by *confidence*? We mean that we have a certain degree of faith that the method will work when we choose to use it, since it works about 95% of the time.

Confidence Intervals

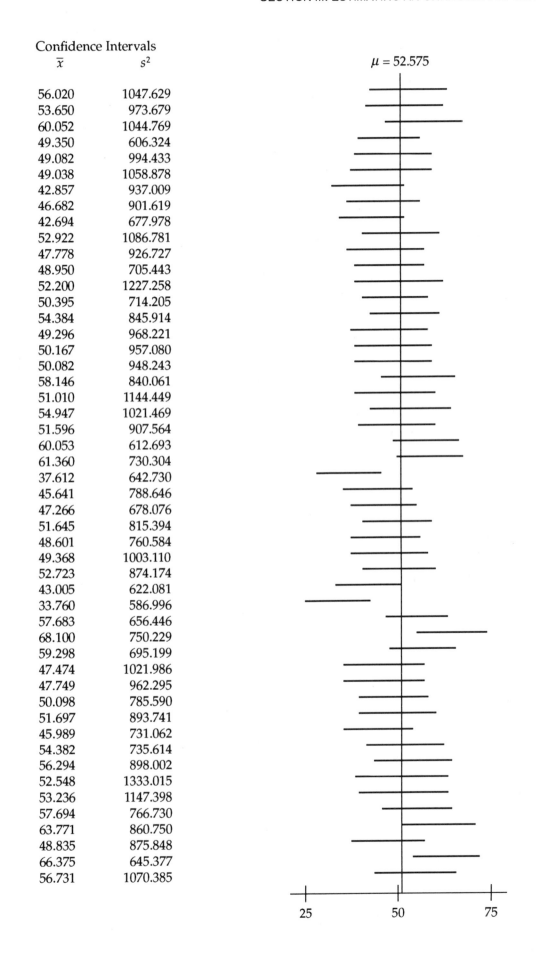

$\overline{x}$	s^2
56.020	1047.629
53.650	973.679
60.052	1044.769
49.350	606.324
49.082	994.433
49.038	1058.878
42.857	937.009
46.682	901.619
42.694	677.978
52.922	1086.781
47.778	926.727
48.950	705.443
52.200	1227.258
50.395	714.205
54.384	845.914
49.296	968.221
50.167	957.080
50.082	948.243
58.146	840.061
51.010	1144.449
54.947	1021.469
51.596	907.564
60.053	612.693
61.360	730.304
37.612	642.730
45.641	788.646
47.266	678.076
51.645	815.394
48.601	760.584
49.368	1003.110
52.723	874.174
43.005	622.081
33.760	586.996
57.683	656.446
68.100	750.229
59.298	695.199
47.474	1021.986
47.749	962.295
50.098	785.590
51.697	893.741
45.989	731.062
54.382	735.614
56.294	898.002
52.548	1333.015
53.236	1147.398
57.694	766.730
63.771	860.750
48.835	875.848
66.375	645.377
56.731	1070.385

$\mu = 52.575$

1. A traffic engineer estimates the average number of cars per hour passing through 20 different intersections in a city by observing traffic for random samples of hours from each intersection. He constructs separate 95%-confidence-interval estimates for each intersection. Would you expect all 20 confidence intervals to include the true mean hourly rate? How many would you expect to not include the true hourly rate? Can you tell which ones may not include the true hourly rate?

2. Working in groups, select 40 samples, each with $n = 10$ random digits, from a random number table. Construct 40 confidence intervals for the true mean value of the digits in a random number table, which is 4.5. How many of the 40 intervals do not include the true mean? Is this surprising?

3. How does the pattern in amount of precipitation (rainfall) across the Southeast change with month? The following data show typical values for monthly total precipitation (in inches) for 18 weather stations scattered across the region of interest. These 18 data points can be thought of as a sample of typical measurements for any particular month. A plot of all this data would not give a very clear picture of the pattern. To clarify the picture, we could use the data from each month to produce a confidence-interval estimate of the true mean precipitation across the region for that month. These intervals, with the sample mean marked at the center, would then show the pattern across months as well as a measure of variation within the months. To illustrate for January, the sample mean ($\bar{x}$) is 3.79 and the standard deviation (s) across cities is 0.92. The confidence-interval estimate for the true January mean is the following:

$$\bar{x} \pm 2\frac{s}{\sqrt{n}}$$

$$= 3.79 \pm 0.43$$

$$= (3.36, 4.22)$$

This interval is plotted on a graph, along with the means for all 12 months.

a. Complete the graph of the data summary by constructing confidence intervals for the remaining months.

b. Which months have the most rainfall? Which have the least?

c. Which months seem to have the most variation in rainfall across the region? Which have the least?

d. Write a description of the pattern you see here.

City	Jan	Feb	Mar	Apr	May	June	July	Aug	Sep	Oct	Nov	Dec
Asheville, NC	3.5	3.6	5.1	3.8	4.2	4.2	4.4	4.8	4.0	3.3	3.3	3.5
Atlanta, GA	4.9	4.4	5.9	4.4	4.0	3.4	4.7	3.4	3.2	2.5	3.4	4.2
Birmingham, AL	5.2	4.7	6.6	5.0	4.5	3.7	5.4	3.9	4.3	2.7	3.6	5.0
Charleston, SC	3.3	3.4	4.4	2.6	4.4	6.5	7.3	6.5	4.9	2.9	2.2	3.1
Jackson, MS	5.0	4.9	5.9	5.9	4.8	2.9	4.4	3.7	3.6	2.6	4.2	5.4
Jacksonville, FL	3.1	3.5	3.7	3.3	4.9	5.4	6.5	7.2	7.3	3.4	1.9	2.6
Knoxville, TN	4.7	4.2	5.5	3.9	3.7	4.0	4.3	3.0	3.0	2.7	3.8	4.6
Lexington, KY	3.6	3.3	4.8	4.0	4.2	4.3	5.0	4.0	3.3	2.3	3.3	3.8
Louisville, KY	3.4	3.2	4.7	4.1	4.2	3.6	4.1	3.3	3.6	2.6	3.5	3.5
Memphis, TN	4.6	4.3	5.4	5.8	5.1	3.6	4.0	3.7	3.6	2.4	4.2	4.9
Miami, FL	2.1	2.1	1.9	3.1	6.5	9.2	6.0	7.0	8.1	7.1	2.7	1.9
Mobile, AL	4.6	4.9	6.5	5.4	5.5	5.1	7.7	6.8	6.6	2.6	3.7	5.4
Nashville, TN	4.5	4.0	5.6	4.8	4.6	3.7	3.8	3.4	3.7	2.6	3.5	4.6
Norfolk, VA	3.7	3.3	3.9	2.9	3.8	3.5	5.2	5.3	4.4	3.4	2.9	3.2
Raleigh, NC	3.6	3.4	3.7	2.9	3.7	3.7	4.4	4.4	3.3	2.7	2.9	3.1
Richmond, VA	3.2	3.1	3.6	2.9	3.6	3.6	5.1	5.0	3.5	3.7	3.3	3.4
Savannah, GA	3.1	3.2	3.8	3.2	4.6	5.7	7.4	6.7	5.2	2.3	1.9	2.8
Tampa, FL	2.2	3.0	3.5	1.8	3.4	5.3	7.4	7.6	6.2	2.3	1.9	2.1

Source: *1992 World Almanac*, p. 207.

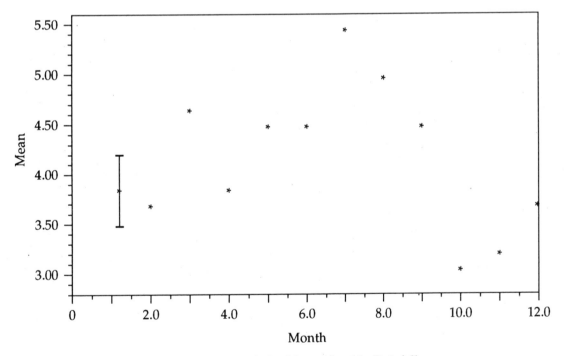

Confidence Intervals for Mean Monthly Rainfall

Using Averages to Estimate Areas

Engineers are many times required to estimate the area or volume of an irregular shape. One of the techniques involves finding the average width.

To estimate the area of an irregular shape,

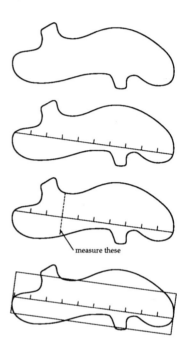

a. Draw a line segment to represent the length of the figure.

b. Divide the length into a convenient number of division points, at least ten.

c. Measure the width at each division point perpendicular to the length.

d. Calculate the average width (our estimate of the area is length times average width).

e. Draw the rectangle which we are using to approximate the area of the irregular shape.

The confidence-interval estimate of the true area can be found by doing the following:

a. Form a confidence-interval estimate of the average width using the sample measurements and the techniques of this section.

b. Multiply both ends of the confidence interval by the length of the figure.

Calculate a 95%-confidence-interval estimate of the area of the figure given above. Compare your answer to those of other students.

Below is a scale drawing of a golf green. One centimeter on the drawing corresponds to 1 meter on the actual green. What is the area of the green?

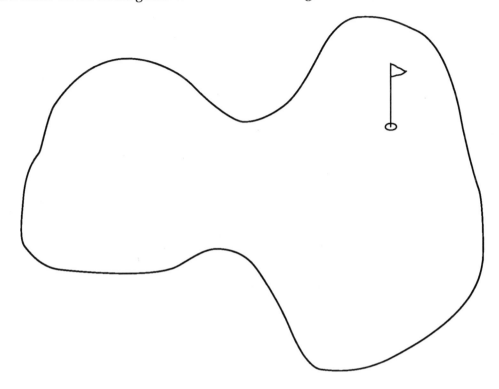

Below is a photograph of the area burned by a forest fire. One centimeter in the photograph corresponds to 1.5 kilometers on the ground. Estimate the area burned.

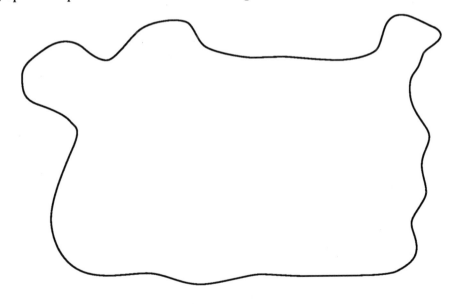

Let's see how the concepts we've learned so far might help us with a physical-measurement problem in the physics laboratory. A group of high-school students measured the acceleration of a falling body by using three different devices:

a.　A free-fall machine in which the acceleration is a function of the distance and time of a falling ball.

b.　An inclined plane in which the acceleration is a function of the distance traversed by a glider down the plane, the height of the plane, and the time.

c.　A pendulum in which the acceleration is a function of the length of the pendulum and the time of a vibration.

The data obtained on acceleration due to gravity are given below (in m/sec^2).

Trial	Free Fall	Inclined Plane	Pendulum
1	9.97	10.90	10.18
2	9.84	10.65	10.08
3	9.80	11.37	9.78
4	9.81	10.06	9.83
5	9.80	10.16	10.13
6	9.80	10.16	9.95
7	9.81	9.76	9.82
8	9.81	10.55	10.12
9	9.88	10.30	9.96
10	9.97	10.05	9.97
11	9.78	10.76	9.80
12	9.81	10.31	9.81
13	9.78	10.76	9.80
14	9.80	9.91	9.73
15	9.87	9.25	9.82
16	9.81	10.13	9.84

Source: Maher and Pancari, *Teaching Statistics*, 12, No. 2, Summer 1990, pp. 34–37.

1.　Explore the three data sets by making appropriate plots and calculating appropriate summary statistics. Write a paragraph describing the data.

2.　The inclined plain seems to give higher readings than the other methods. (A systematic higher or lower reading of a measuring device is called *bias*. Your bathroom scale is *biased* if you set it five pounds below the zero mark when no one is on it.) Can you think of a cause of the bias on the inclined plane?

3. Produce a confidence-interval estimate of the true acceleration due to gravity from each of the three samples. How do they compare with one another?

4. Which method of measuring acceleration do you prefer? Why?

5. If you are in a physics class, or have access to a laboratory, repeat this experiment and analyze your results.

Application 30

Find a good road map of the state of Florida, or your home state, if you prefer. Identify the county boundaries on the map. Also, identify lakes, usually shown in blue. Our goal is to estimate the number of lakes in Florida (of a size large enough to be shown on a map).

1. Randomly choose five counties from the state map.

2. Count the number of lakes in each county. If more than half a lake is in the county under study, count it.

3. Form a confidence-interval estimate of the mean number of lakes per county.

4. Multiply each end of the confidence interval by the number of counties (67 for Florida) to obtain an interval estimate of the number of lakes in the state.

Summary

Data collected in the form of measurements (heights, weights, lengths, areas, time intervals) are inherently different from data collected in the form of frequency counts or proportions (proportion of males, proportion who have jobs, proportion of foreign autos). For measurement data, the goal of the analysis is to do the following:

a. Describe the distribution of the data over the real number line.

b. Summarize key features of the data such as center and variability.

If the data come through random sampling of a fixed population, then a third goal is the following:

c. Estimate appropriate population parameters.

Section I of *Exploring Measurements* considers appropriate graphical and numerical descriptions of measurement data. Two common measures of center are the mean and median; two common measures of variability are the interquartile range and the standard deviation. The mean and standard deviation are good measures of center and spread (variability) for mound-shaped, approximately symmetric distributions. Otherwise, the median and interquartile range may provide more useful summaries.

Section II shows that the possible values a sample mean can assume in repeated sampling possess a mound-shaped, symmetrical distribution (called a sampling distribution). Thus, properties of the sample mean and the sample standard deviation are useful in describing the behavior of the sample mean as an estimator of the corresponding population mean. Through simulation, we can arrive at a theoretical expression for the standard deviation of the sampling distribution of sample means. This helps us describe the potential values of a sample mean in any sampling situation involving measurement data.

Section III shows that by making use of the distribution of potential values of a sample mean (the sampling distribution), we can estimate an unknown population mean. In other words, from a single sample we can decide which of the many possible values for an unknown population mean are consistent with the sample results. The resulting consistent set of possible values for the population mean is called a confidence interval. Making decisions through the construction of confidence intervals is not foolproof; we can be wrong. But the approach is a logical one that will lead to the correct decision more often than can be achieved by guessing.

We hope that you now have a deeper awareness of how to collect and analyze measurement data and an awareness of the role of randomization in collecting samples. We hope that this awareness makes you more alert to the ways in which data are used and misused in the world around you. In addition, we hope you have gained a broader perspective of the importance and usefulness of mathematics as an essential tool for solving real problems.